Level D

Shoreview, Minnesota

AMP™ *QReads*™ is based upon the instructional routine developed by **Elfrieda (Freddy) H. Hiebert** (Ph.D., University of Wisconsin—Madison). Professor Hiebert is Adjunct Professor at the University of California, Berkeley and has been a classroom teacher, university-based teacher, and educator for over 35 years. She has published over 130 research articles and chapters in journals and books on how instruction and materials influence reading acquisition. Professor Hiebert's TExT model for accessible texts has been used to develop widely-used reading programs, including *QuickReads*® and *QuickReads*® *Technology* (Pearson Learning Group).

The publisher wishes to thank the following educators for their helpful comments during the review process for *AMP*™ *QReads*™. Their assistance has been invaluable:

Shelley Al-Khatib, Teacher, Life Skills, Chippewa Middle School, North Oaks, MN; **Ann Ertl,** ESL Department Lead, Champlin Park High School, Champlin, MN; **Dr. Kathleen Sullivan,** Supervisor, Reading Services Center, Omaha Public Schools, Omaha, NE; **Ryan E. Summers,** Teacher, English, Neelsville Middle School, Germantown, MD.

Acknowledgments appear on page 176, which constitutes an extension of this copyright page.

ISBN-13: 978-0-7854-6305-4
ISBN-10: 0-7854-6305-4

1 2 3 4 5 6 7 8 9 10   11 10 09 08 07

PEARSON
AGS Globe

1-800-992-0244
www.agsglobe.com

CONTENTS

Social Studies

Literature and Language

Science

Arts and Culture

Welcome to QReads™!

Please follow these steps for each page of readings:

FIRST READ

1. Read the Fast Facts and think about what you might already know about the topic. Look for two words that are new or difficult. Draw a line under these words.

2. Read the page aloud or silently to yourself. Always include the title at the top of the same page. Take as much time as you need.

3. Find the first page in Building Connections. Write some words or phrases there to help you remember what is important.

SECOND READ

1. Listen and read along silently with your teacher or the audio track.

2. Use the target rate of 1 minute when listening and reading along.

3. Ask yourself, what is one thing to remember? Answer the Key Notes question to help find what is important.

THIRD READ

1. Now, try to read as much of the page as you can within 1 minute.

2. Read silently as you are timed for 1 minute. Read aloud with a partner or your teacher. Circle the last word you read at the end of 1 minute.

3. Write down the number of words you read on the page. Review in your mind what is important to remember.

4. Complete the questions or other reading given by your teacher.

Immigration to the United States

These photos at Ellis Island show immigrants to the United States.

Fast Facts

- About 12 percent of the people who live in the United States were born in other countries.

- More immigrants come to the United States from Mexico than from any other country.

- About 1.5 percent of U.S. citizens today are American Indians.

A Land of Immigrants

Immigrants are people who leave their home country to live in a new country. Except for American Indians, every[23] U.S. citizen has a family member who was once an immigrant to the United States. Some families have lived in this country[45] for hundreds of years and do not think of themselves as immigrants. Others may be either immigrants themselves or the children of immigrants.[68]

People come to the United States from many countries. Many immigrants come looking for new opportunities.[84] While some seek better jobs, others seek opportunities to live their lives as they wish. Living as they wish is an opportunity that people may not have in other countries.[114]

KEY NOTES

A Land of Immigrants
Why do immigrants come to the United States?

_____

_____

Immigration to the United States

Travel on ships to the United States was difficult for immigrants.

Fast Facts

- About 500,000 Africans were brought to North America as slaves before 1860.

- A ticket for the bottom deck of a ship might cost $25, about two years' wages.

- Up to 2,000 people fit in the bottom deck; ship companies could earn up to $65,000 for each group of immigrants.

Getting to the United States

Until about 50 years ago, most immigrants came to the United States in ships. The conditions on these early ship[25] voyages were difficult, especially for the people who were brought from Africa as slaves. Even for immigrants who chose[44] to come to the United States, though, these voyages could be hard.[56]

Between 1900 and 1920, 13 million immigrants arrived in ships from Europe. Many of these people, especially the poor,[75] traveled in very difficult conditions. Many immigrants could only pay to travel on the bottom decks of ships, which were[95] often crowded and windowless. Today, however, most immigrants to the United States arrive by plane.[110]

KEY NOTES

Getting to the United States   What was life like for immigrants who traveled to the United States between 1900 and 1920?

_____

_____

Immigration to the United States

Immigrants cheer as their ship comes into New York Harbor, about 1900.

Fast Facts

- From 1892 to 1954, about 12 million immigrants landed at Ellis Island.

- Almost half of all Americans can trace their roots to someone who landed at Ellis Island.

- From 1910 to 1940, about 175,000 Chinese immigrants landed at Angel Island.

Ellis and Angel Islands

After 1886, the Statue of Liberty greeted ships arriving in New York. Immigrants often cheered when they saw the [23] Statue of Liberty. Many of these immigrants passed through Ellis Island. [34]

First, immigrants were given medical checks to be sure they were well. Some people who were ill were sent back to [55] their home country. People who passed their medical check were questioned about their background. Finally, immigrants were told if they could stay in the United States. [81]

Immigrants who arrived on the West Coast were checked at Angel Island in California. Most of these immigrants came [100] from China. Some were kept at Angel Island for as long as two years. [114]

KEY NOTES
Ellis and Angel Islands   What was the first thing that happened to immigrants on Ellis and Angel Islands?
_____
_____

Immigration to the United States

Immigrants study English to pass a test to become a U.S. citizen.

Fast Facts

- More than 450,000 people become U.S citizens each year.

- One question on the citizenship test has been, "What are the colors of our flag?"

- American Indians did not become U.S. citizens until 1924.

Becoming a U.S. Citizen

Most Americans become citizens by being born in the United States. However, every year more than 700,000 [21] immigrants come to this country. Many come because they want to become U.S. citizens. [35]

Before 1906, people were not required to know English to become U.S. citizens. Since then, laws were changed to require [55] those who want to become citizens to speak, read, and write English. This requirement means that many new citizens speak [75] more than one language. People who want to become citizens also must pass a test about the history and laws of the United [98] States. Today, only people who know English and pass this test can become U.S. citizens. [113]

KEY NOTES

Becoming a U.S. Citizen

What must immigrants know to become U.S. citizens?

_____

_____

Immigration to the United States

A Land of Immigrants

1. The main idea of "A Land of Immigrants" is that _____

    a. everyone who lives in a country is an immigrant.
    b. all children in the United States are immigrants.
    c. visitors to the United States are immigrants.
    d. someone in most U.S. families was an immigrant.

2. What is an immigrant?

_____

_____

_____

3. What are two kinds of opportunity people seek when they come to the United States?

_____

_____

_____

Getting to the United States

1. "Getting to the United States" is MAINLY about _____

    a. how much immigrants had to pay to get to the United States.
    b. how difficult it is to get to the United States today.
    c. how immigrants came to the United States years ago and today.
    d. rules for getting to the United States on airplanes.

2. Compare how most immigrants came to the United States about 50 years ago with how they come today.

_____

_____

_____

3. Why were conditions on the ships difficult for many immigrants from Africa and from Europe?

_____

_____

_____

Ellis and Angel Islands

1. Another good name for "Ellis and Angel Islands" is _____

    a. "The Statue of Liberty."
    b. "Why Immigrants Came to the United States."
    c. "Living at Ellis Island."
    d. "Arriving in the United States."

2. Immigrants were checked to be sure _____

    a. they could speak English.
    b. they were not ill.
    c. they had enough money.
    d. they were U.S. citizens.

3. What happened at Ellis and Angel Islands?

_____

_____

_____

Becoming a U.S. Citizen

1. Many immigrants to the United States want to _____

    a. become U.S. citizens.
    b. go to Ellis Island.
    c. visit the United States.
    d. learn how to be immigrants.

2. In 1906, how did laws change that allowed immigrants to become U.S. citizens?

    a. Fewer people were allowed to become citizens.
    b. Immigrants had to know English.
    c. More people had to become citizens.
    d. Immigrants had to become citizens.

3. What are two things immigrants need to do today to become citizens?

_____

_____

_____

immigrants	opportunity	conditions	voyages
statue	liberty	citizens	require

1. Choose the word from the word box above that best matches each definition. Write the word on the line below.

A. _____ being free

B. _____ a chance to do something new

C. _____ a figure of a person or animal

D. _____ the way things are

E. _____ people who move to a new country to make a new home

F. _____ need to have or do something

G. _____ trips

H. _____ people who are members of a country

2. Fill in the blanks in the sentences below. Choose the word from the word box that completes each sentence.

A. My town put up a _____ of the person who started the town.

B. My parents came to the United States to become _____.

C. It was cold, so the _____ for swimming were not good.

D. The school will _____ new students to pass a test to move to the next grade.

E. If you are free, you have the _____ to do what you want.

F. The United States is sometimes called the land of _____ because people can do many things here.

G. More _____ come to a country when more jobs are available.

H. I like _____ by sea because I have always loved boats.

Immigration to the United States

1. Use the idea web to help you remember what you read. In each box, write the main idea of that reading.

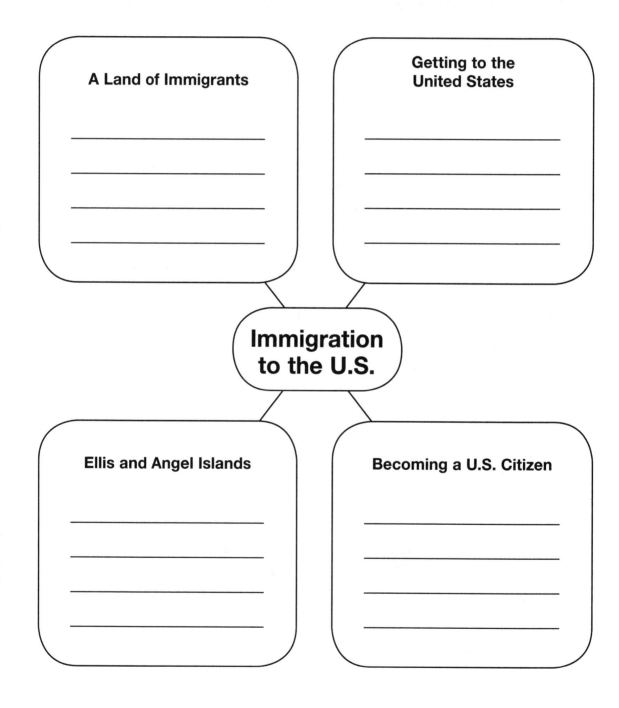

A Land of Immigrants

Getting to the United States

Immigration to the U.S.

Ellis and Angel Islands

Becoming a U.S. Citizen

2. How do you think immigrants changed the United States?

_____

_____

_____

_____

3. What are three things immigrants might have to do differently in a new country?

_____

_____

_____

_____

4. Why do you think immigrants come to the United States today?

_____

_____

_____

_____

Our North American Neighbors

People enter the United States at this border crossing in Canada.

Fast Facts

- The border between Mexico and the United States is about 1,500 miles long.

- The border between Canada and the United States is about 4,000 miles long.

- Alaska, a state in the United States, has a little less land than all of Mexico.

Three North American Countries

The United States is in North America. Canada is its northern neighbor, and Mexico is its southern neighbor.[22]

With almost 4 million square miles, Canada is the second-largest country in the world. However, Canada has only about[42] 30 million people. In contrast, although Mexico has only about one-fifth the land area of Canada, it has about 100 million people.[65]

The United States has less land area than Canada but more than Mexico. In 2002, almost 300 million people lived in the[87] United States. That means that the United States has about ten times more people than Canada and about three times more people than Mexico.[111]

KEY NOTES

Three North American Countries

How are Canada, Mexico, and the United States different in size?

_____

_____

Our North American Neighbors

The Canadian Rockies in Alberta are known for their beauty.

Fast Facts

- American Indians lived in both North and South America before settlers came from other countries.

- There are 535 representatives in the United States Congress.

- There are 405 representatives in Canada's national government.

Comparing Canada and the United States

Canada and the United States are similar in many ways. Both countries stretch for thousands of miles. The Rocky Mountains and the Great Plains are in the middle of both countries.[37]

Most people in both countries speak English because many of the settlers came from England. Canada also had many[56] settlers from France. In some parts of Canada, most people speak French. Many signs in Canada are in both English and French.[78]

People in both the United States and Canada elect representatives to govern them. However, the two countries[95] choose their leaders differently. While people in the United States elect a president, Canada's elected representatives choose its leader.[114]

KEY NOTES

Comparing Canada and the United States   How do the people of the United States and Canada choose their leaders?

_____

_____

Our North American Neighbors

This park in Mexico City is full of history.

Fast Facts

- Mexico has more people than any other Spanish-speaking country in the world.

- The name *Mexico* comes from one of the country's native people.

- At its narrowest point, Mexico is 125 miles across.

Mexico and Its North American Neighbors

Compared to the land area of Canada and the United States, Mexico's land area is small. At some points, Mexico's east and[28] west coasts are close together. However, traveling in Mexico can be difficult because the country has mountain ranges near both[48] coasts. Therefore, most of Mexico's population lives in the center of the country, where travel is easier.[65]

Although most of the population of Canada and the United States speaks English, most of Mexico's population speaks[83] Spanish. That is because many of Mexico's settlers were from Spain. Also, because Mexico is the farthest south, the temperature is warmer there than in the rest of North America.[113]

KEY NOTES

Mexico and Its North American Neighbors
Why do some people in Mexico speak Spanish?

_____

_____

Our North American Neighbors

The Aztec people built Mexico City.

Fast Facts

- Mexico City has the largest population of any city in North America.

- Mexico City was founded by the Aztecs almost 700 years ago.

- Mexico City is more than 570 square miles in area.

Mexico City

Mexico's capital, Mexico City, is the oldest city in North America. When the Spanish arrived in North America more[21] than 450 years ago, they found a city already located there. People called the Aztecs had built the city, which had some[43] large pyramids. Today, visitors from around the world go to see the Aztec pyramids.[57]

Mexico City is also famous for its size and height. It is the second-largest city in the world. More than 25 million people,[81] or about one-fifth of the Mexican population, live there. Mexico City is also the highest city in North America. It is almost one and one-half miles above sea level.[112]

KEY NOTES

Mexico City   What did the Spanish settlers find when they arrived in North America?

_____

_____

Our North American Neighbors

Three North American Countries

1. Another good name for "Three North American Countries"
is _____

    a. "Canada and the United States."
    b. "The People of North America."
    c. "North American Neighbors."
    d. "The Many Countries of Canada."

2. Which country in North America is largest in land area? Which
country is smallest?

_____

_____

_____

3. Which country in North America has the most people? Which
country has the fewest?

_____

_____

_____

Comparing Canada and the United States

1. "Comparing Canada and the United States" is MAINLY
about _____

    a. how much larger the United States is than Canada.
    b. the governments of the United States and Canada.
    c. the people who settled the United States and Canada.
    d. ways Canada and the United States are alike and different.

2. Name two ways in which Canada and the United States are similar.

_____

_____

_____

3. Name two ways in which Canada and the United States are different.

_____

_____

_____

Mexico and Its North American Neighbors

1. Which of the following is a fact about Mexico?

   a. Mexico is smaller than its North American neighbors.
   b. Most of the people in Mexico live near its coasts.
   c. Mexico is larger than its North American neighbors.
   d. Most of Mexico's settlers came from England.

2. Where do most Mexicans live?

   a. on the coasts
   b. in the mountains near Canada
   c. in the center of the country
   d. near the United States

3. Describe two ways Mexico is different from Canada and the United States.

_____

_____

_____

Mexico City

a. the people in Mexico City who speak Spanish.
b. some reasons Mexico City is famous.
c. the Aztec pyramids in Mexico City.
d. the size and height of Mexico City.

2. List three facts about Mexico City.

_____

_____

_____

3. Who were the Aztecs? What had they built before the Spanish arrived in North America?

_____

_____

_____

Canada	Mexico	Aztec	population
neighbor	pyramids	representatives	

1. Choose the word from the word box above that best matches each definition. Write the word on the line below.

A. _____ a person who lives near other people

B. _____ the country that lies north of the United States

C. _____ the number of people who live in a place

D. _____ the country that lies south of the United States

E. _____ buildings with four slanting sides that meet in a point at the top

F. _____ relating to a group of people who lived in Mexico before the Spanish settlers arrived

G. _____ people who speak and act for others

2. Fill in the blanks in the sentences below. Choose the word from the word box that completes each sentence.

A. The _____ of our city grew when new houses were built.

B. The country of _____ lies south of the United States.

C. The pointed shape of the _____ made them easy to see.

D. We have a nice _____ living in the house next door.

E. Because _____ lies north of the United States, it is colder there.

F. The _____ people built pyramids and cities in the area that became Mexico.

G. We elect our government's _____.

33

Our North American Neighbors

1. In the central area labeled All 3 Countries, write how the three North American countries are alike. Write how they are different in each country's circle.

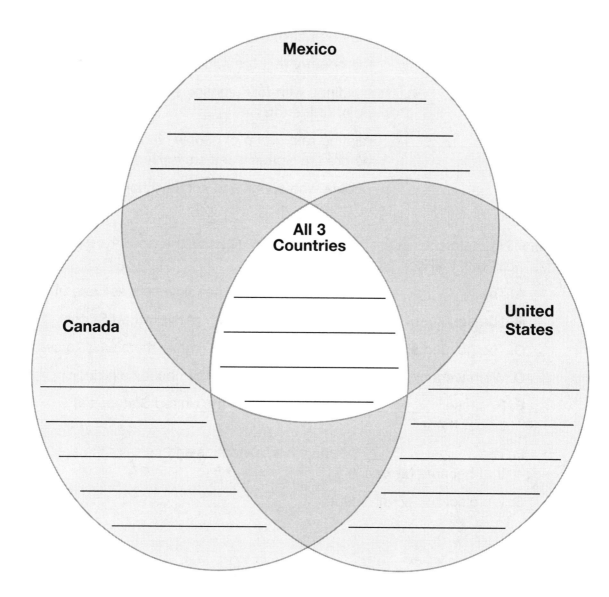

2. How is the weather in Mexico different from the weather in Canada? Explain your answer.

_____

_____

_____

_____

3. How do you think settlers might change a country?

_____

_____

_____

_____

4. Suppose there was another reading in this topic. Do you think it would be about North American maps or governments? Explain your answer.

_____

_____

_____

_____

Ancient Rome

Ancient buildings in Rome can still be seen on the hills.

Fast Facts

- Ancient Rome was founded in about 753 B.C.

- The Roman Empire lasted more than 1,000 years.

- The word *citizen* comes from the Latin word for *city*.

Rome in Ancient Times

Today, Rome is a beautiful city in Italy. However, Rome was already important in ancient times. It was located on seven hills,[26] so it was possible for the early Romans to see their enemies coming from miles away. As a result, Rome was able to prepare[50] for enemy attacks. From its secure location, Rome built an empire that ruled a large part of the world.[69]

Ancient Rome was unusual because it offered citizenship to many of its people. Rome's citizens had certain rights and[88] were protected by its laws. However, although Rome gave many people citizenship, it still permitted its citizens to force others into slavery.[110]

KEY NOTES

Rome in Ancient Times
What was Rome like in ancient times?

_____

_____

Ancient Rome

The Roman army added new places to the empire.

Fast Facts

- Roman soldiers had to sign up for 25 years in the army.

- Roman soldiers marched 20 miles a day carrying packs that weighed as much as 90 pounds.

- Roman soldiers marched into battle standing shoulder to shoulder in straight rows.

The Roman Army

The Roman army was one reason the Roman Empire stayed strong. Like their enemies, Roman soldiers had only swords,[22] spears, and heavy armor to protect them. What made the Roman army different, though, was its organization. The Roman army[42] was organized into a large group that was then divided into smaller and smaller groups. Each group in this organization had strong leaders.[65]

The Roman army was also different in that it did not destroy the places it conquered. Instead, the places were added[86] to the Roman Empire. With every place the army conquered, the Roman Empire grew. At its largest, the Roman Empire included large parts of Europe and Africa.[113]

KEY NOTES

The Roman Army
How was the Roman army different from other armies?

_____

_____

Ancient Rome

This aqueduct in France was built by ancient Romans.

Fast Facts

- Many ancient Roman roads are still used in Europe today.

- The Romans built 50,000 miles of stone roads.

- Aqueducts carried 38 million gallons of water every day into ancient Rome.

Roman Engineering

The saying "All roads lead to Rome" refers to the system of roads built by ancient Roman engineers. Roads made of solid[24] stone ran to all parts of the empire. These roads made it easier to control the empire because people could travel quickly.[46]

Roman engineers also built other structures that can still be seen in Europe today. They built bridges across rivers.[65] When cities needed water, Roman engineers built aqueducts. Aqueducts are huge stone pipes that carried water from lakes[83] and rivers to cities. Roman engineers built cities in the lands they conquered, too. Some cities were built on a grid, making it easy for people to get around.[112]

KEY NOTES

Roman Engineering
What did ancient Roman engineers build?

_____

_____

Ancient Rome

Children in ancient Rome learned the same skills as those of their parents.

Fast Facts

- Ancient Romans thought it was bad manners to eat their meals sitting up, so they ate lying on their sides.

- Children in ancient Rome went to school *every* day. Breaks were on holidays.

- Roman sports included games like today's handball, soccer, and field hockey.

Daily Life in Ancient Rome

As is often the case, life was easier for rich people in ancient Rome than it was for poor people. Poor Roman families lived in[30] apartments that had two or three rooms. These apartments were in large buildings. In contrast, rich Roman families had huge houses and many servants.[54]

Some children of rich Roman families went to private schools. There was no school for other children, who usually[73] worked in their family's business. For example, if the members of a family were cloth merchants, the children became cloth[93] merchants, too. Because they didn't learn new skills, most Roman families lived the same way for many years.[111]

KEY NOTES

Daily Life in Ancient Rome
How did rich and poor Roman families live?

_____

_____

Ancient Rome

Rome in Ancient Times

1. How did Rome's location help its people?

a. Rome was located in the country of Italy.
b. The Romans could see their enemies coming from far away.
c. Rome was able to see many other countries.
d. The Romans could have rights and become citizens.

2. Which of these is a fact about ancient Rome?

a. Ancient Rome offered citizenship to many people.
b. Ancient Rome was in the United States.
c. Ancient Rome was ruled by other empires.
d. Ancient Rome is an important city today.

3. Retell what you learned in "Rome in Ancient Times."

_____

_____

_____

The Roman Army

1. The main idea of "The Roman Army" is that _____

a. the Roman army conquered Europe.
b. the Roman army used guns and heavy armor.
c. the Roman army destroyed the places it conquered.
d. the Roman army was different from other armies.

2. How was the Roman army organized?

_____

_____

_____

3. What did the Roman government do when its soldiers conquered
a place?

_____

_____

_____

Roman Engineering

1. Another good name for "Roman Engineering" is _____

    a. "Ancient Roman Bridges."
    b. "Jobs in Ancient Rome."
    c. "Ancient Roman Building."
    d. "How Ancient Romans Built Cities."

2. Ancient Roman roads _____

    a. helped people get around easily.
    b. were built over aqueducts.
    c. helped engineers build grids.
    d. were only used by its citizens.

3. Describe two things ancient Roman engineers built.

_____

_____

_____

Daily Life in Ancient Rome

1. In ancient Rome, _____

    a. both rich and poor children went to school.
    b. life was easier for rich people than for poor people.
    c. most people lived in large apartments.
    d. only the rich were cloth merchants.

2. Why did the children of poor people work in their family's business?

_____

_____

_____

3. Describe two ways in which rich Romans lived differently from poor Romans.

_____

_____

_____

citizenship	location	organization	aqueducts
engineer	apartments	merchants	conquered

1. Choose the word from the word box above that best matches each definition. Write the word on the line below.

A. _____ got something by using force

B. _____ the place where something is

C. _____ someone who plans or builds machines, roads, and bridges

D. _____ being a member of a particular country, city, or town

E. _____ people who sell things

F. _____ one or more rooms that people live in inside a larger building

G. _____ huge stone bridges with pipes that carry water to people

H. _____ putting things together in an orderly way

2. Fill in the blanks in the sentences below. Choose the word from the word box that completes each sentence.

A. The _____ of the school gym makes it easy to leave after practice.

B. Our town needs an _____ to design a new bridge.

C. The library has an _____ that helps me find books easily.

D. The _____ who sell milk get it fresh from the farms every day.

E. James's family lives in a large building that has many

_____.

F. One of the rights of _____ is the ability to vote.

G. The big stone _____ carried water to Rome from many miles away.

H. When the Roman army _____ an enemy, it allowed some people to have rights.

47

Ancient Rome

1. Use the idea web to help you remember what you read. In each box, write the main idea of that reading. Then, use that information to write the main idea of the topic in the central box.

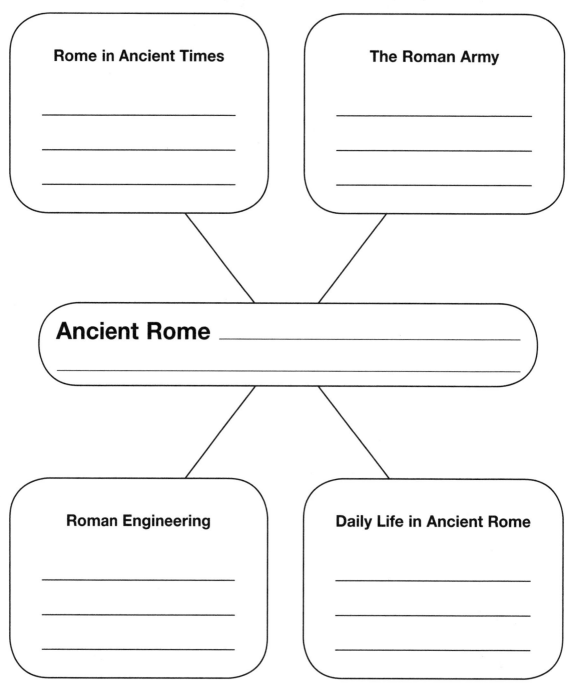

Rome in Ancient Times

_____

_____

_____

The Roman Army

_____

_____

_____

Ancient Rome _____

_____

Roman Engineering

_____

_____

_____

Daily Life in Ancient Rome

_____

_____

_____

48

2. Name three ways life in ancient Rome was similar to life in the United States today.

_____

_____

_____

_____

3. Name three ways the Roman Empire was different from other ancient countries.

_____

_____

_____

_____

4. Suppose there was another reading in this topic. Do you think it would be about what life is like in Rome today or the clothes people wore in ancient Rome? Explain.

_____

_____

_____

_____

Mystery Writing

Mystery novels by this writer, Agatha Christie, asked a question: "Who did it?"

Fast Facts

- In a "locked room" mystery, a dead person is found in what seems to be a sealed room.

- Almost 25 percent of the books adults buy to read are mysteries.

- Books by Agatha Christie, a mystery writer, have sold about 2 billion copies.

What Is Mystery Writing?

The door creaks and slowly opens. Readers catch their breath. Anything could be on the other side of that door. In[25] mystery writing, that is the point. The thrill is in the *suspense*, or not knowing what will happen.[43]

Mystery stories often have riddles to solve. Sometimes, a person may be trying to find the answer to the question, "Who[64] did it?" The reader travels with that person as he or she looks for clues and solves the crime.[83]

In addition to feelings of suspense, the feeling of danger is an important part of a mystery. The reader reads on, thrilled[105] by the danger the person in the novel faces. In mystery writing, the ending is often a surprise.[123]

KEY NOTES

What Is Mystery Writing?
What can happen in mystery stories?

_____

_____

Mystery Writing

The character of Sherlock Holmes, a detective, is in many mystery books.

Fast Facts

- Mystery stories have been made into radio programs, TV shows, and movies.

- Some bookstores sell only mysteries; one has more than 15,000 titles.

- Some hotels have crime-solving weekends, where guests play detective and try to solve a mystery.

Mystery History

Riddles have been a part of storytelling since ancient times. Some ancient Greek authors of plays included elements of[21] mystery in their works. However, most people trace the modern mystery to the work of Edgar Allan Poe. One of his short stories,[44] which appeared in 1841, is called the first modern mystery because it had a riddle, clues, and a detective who solved a crime.[67]

Since then, many kinds of mysteries have been bestsellers. Popular mysteries have been written about New York City police[86] detectives and sweet older people who solve crimes in English towns. Several authors have even written about cat detectives[105] that help solve crimes. Mystery books are one of the most popular kinds of fiction today.[121]

KEY NOTES

Mystery History
What kinds of mysteries are popular today?

_____

_____

Mystery Writing

This bird, a raven, is written about in a poem by Edgar Allan Poe.

Fast Facts

- Edgar Allan Poe's famous poem "The Raven" earned him less than $20.

- A pro football team from the city where Poe lived is called the Ravens, after the poem.

- Every year since 1949, a mysterious man has visited Poe's grave on his birthday, and left three roses.

Edgar Allan Poe

Edgar Allan Poe had a hard childhood. His mother died when he was young and he was moved from place to place.[25] He was later kicked out of school. Poe then wrote poetry for magazines and worked as a magazine editor. After his first[47] mystery story was printed in 1841, Poe wrote many more stories.[58]

Poe also wrote poetry. One of his best-known poems is "The Raven," a haunting poem about lost love that was printed in 1845.[82]

Poe wrote poetry and short stories for the rest of his life. His death is a mystery, too. Poe died after stumbling around[105] the streets, wearing someone else's clothes. No one knows what happened to him on that mysterious night.[122]

KEY NOTES

Edgar Allan Poe
What did Edgar Allan Poe write?

_____

_____

Mystery Writing

Edgar Allan Poe wrote a scary story called "The Tell-Tale Heart."

Fast Facts

- Edgar Allan Poe earned $10 for "The Tell-Tale Heart."

- Several movies have been based on "The Tell-Tale Heart."

- The reader never learns the name of the mad narrator in "The Tell-Tale Heart."

"The Tell-Tale Heart"

Edgar Allan Poe's story "The Tell-Tale Heart" is a scary tale. It is the story of a man's growing obsession with an old man[29] who, the narrator admits, has done nothing to him. Readers enter the narrator's strange world of obsession. They see that he can think of nothing but his dislike of the old man.[61]

Part of the mystery of "The Tell-Tale Heart" is in finding out what the narrator will do. As readers follow the story, they[85] notice that the narrator becomes more and more upset. His language becomes more and more odd. By the end, readers[105] understand that the narrator is mad. "The Tell-Tale Heart" is a story not easily forgotten.[121]

KEY NOTES

"The Tell-Tale Heart"

What is the mystery in "The Tell-Tale Heart"?

_____

_____

Mystery Writing

What Is Mystery Writing?

1. "What Is Mystery Writing?" is MAINLY about _____

    a. why people read mystery writing.
    b. how to solve mysteries.
    c. what mysteries are.
    d. how to write a mystery.

2. In mystery writing, _____

    a. the most important thing is the scare.
    b. there is often a riddle to solve.
    c. someone always dies.
    d. the reader usually solves the mystery.

3. What are two things found in mysteries?

_____

_____

_____

Mystery History

1. Who was the first author of a modern mystery story?

_____

_____

_____

2. What do detectives do in a mystery?

    a. make up the mystery
    b. create clues
    c. help others solve the riddle
    d. solve the crime

3. What are two examples of detectives?

_____

_____

_____

Edgar Allan Poe

1. Another good name for "Edgar Allan Poe" is _____

    a. "Master of Mystery."
    b. "The Mystery of the Raven."
    c. "How to Write a Mystery."
    d. "Poetry and Short Stories."

2. Edgar Allan Poe wrote _____

    a. real-life mystery stories.
    b. stories and poems.
    c. books about police officers.
    d. magazines.

3. Why is Edgar Allan Poe's death a mystery?

_____

_____

_____

"The Tell-Tale Heart"

1. This reading is MAINLY about _____

    a. how Poe wrote "The Tell-Tale Heart."
    b. Edgar Allan Poe's life.
    c. a short story called "The Tell-Tale Heart."
    d. how to write a short story.

2. What is the short story "The Tell-Tale Heart" about?

_____

_____

_____

3. How does the narrator of "The Tell-Tale Heart" change in the story?

_____

_____

_____

mystery	suspense	authors	detective
poetry	magazine	obsession	narrator

1. Choose the word from the word box above that best matches each definition. Write the word on the line below.

A. _____ people who write books, stories, plays, or articles

B. _____ a person whose work is to solve crimes

C. _____ an idea that fills a person's thoughts

D. _____ a person who tells what happened in a story

E. _____ a kind of writing that has readers wondering what will happen next

F. _____ a kind of writing that uses special language and may use rhyme

G. _____ a small book that is printed regularly, sometimes every week or month

H. _____ a kind of writing in which there is a secret

2. Fill in the blanks in the sentences below. Choose the word from the word box that completes each sentence.

A. The story she was reading had so much _____ that she jumped when the door opened.

B. That story is a _____ about finding a missing jewel.

C. I get a _____ about cars every month.

D. The _____ is the person who tells the story.

E. Jamie loves puppies so much we think she has an _____ with them.

F. The _____ wrote a book about his childhood.

G. Matthew wrote _____ about nature.

H. The _____ followed the clues to find out who did the crime.

61

Mystery Writing

1. Use the idea web to help you remember what you read. In each box, write the main idea of that reading.

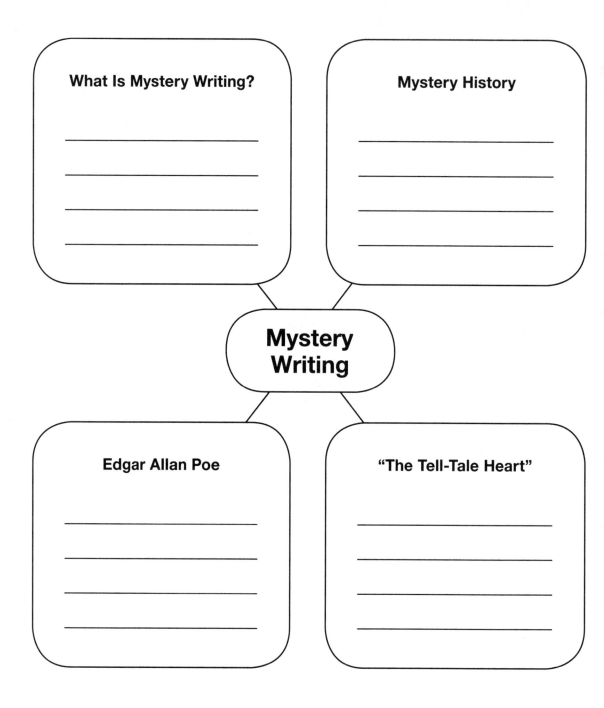

What Is Mystery Writing?

Mystery History

Mystery Writing

Edgar Allan Poe

"The Tell-Tale Heart"

2. What is mystery writing?

_____

_____

_____

_____

3. Why do you think mystery writing is popular today?

_____

_____

_____

_____

4. If you wrote a mystery, what would it be about?

_____

_____

_____

_____

The Internet

The Internet connects people to each other.

Fast Facts

- The word *Internet* was used for the first time in 1982.

- The White House began its Web site in 1993.

- As of 2005, about 1 billion people were using the Internet.

History of the Internet

For many people today, it is hard to imagine life without the Internet. The Internet connects computers around the world,[24] helping people learn information, talk to each other, and buy things.[35]

The Internet began in 1969, when four colleges linked their computers, forming a network. This network allowed people at[54] the colleges and in government to communicate with each other through their computers. It was planned as a way for important people to keep in touch if the United States was attacked.[86]

From that beginning, the Internet grew quickly. In 1976, the queen of England made history by sending an e-mail message[106] through the Internet. By 1996, 45 million people were using their computers to get on the Internet.[123]

KEY NOTES

History of the Internet
Why was the Internet created?

_____

_____

The Internet

E-mail can be sent or read from just about anywhere.

Fast Facts

- A computer engineer invented e-mail in 1971.

- Even the pope has an e-mail address.

- It is estimated that 60 billion e-mail messages will be sent in 2006.

Sending E-Mail

Suppose you want to send an e-mail to a friend. Here is what happens after you type your message and click on Send.[25]

First, the information in your message is broken into small pieces called packets. Each packet is identified by a heading[45] that tells where it came from. The packets are sent separately through a network of computers.[61]

When each packet reaches another computer, it is identified by its heading. Finally, when the message arrives at your[80] friend's computer, the computer collects all the packets of information from your message and puts them back together.[98] Often, the entire process takes only seconds. That's when your friend sees your e-mail message on her computer and can read your news.[121]

Sending E-Mail
What is an e-mail message?

_____

_____

The Internet

Companies that sell on the Internet may also have a store, or not.

Fast Facts

- More than $1.5 trillion in business was done over the Internet in 2003.

- One company sold a jet fighter plane on the Internet for just over $1 million.

- Some Web sites will shop for you, finding all the Internet stores that sell what you want to buy.

Buying and Selling on the Internet

Fifteen years ago, most people had to go to stores to buy things. Today, though, people don't need to leave their home to[29] make a purchase. Instead, they use the Internet to buy and sell everything from hammers to houses.[46]

In the late 1970s, companies used the Internet to send orders and bills. In the 1990s, people began to use the Internet to purchase things directly from a company.[75]

Some companies that sell through the Internet also have stores. Others only sell on the Internet. One Internet-only way[95] of purchasing and selling is to bid on items on a Web site. On these sites, people buy and sell things from each other without ever meeting.[122]

KEY NOTES

Buying and Selling on the Internet   How has the Internet changed the way people buy and sell things?

_____

_____

The Internet

A firewall can stop a virus from entering a computer.

Fast Facts

- There are about 53,000 computer viruses in existence.

- A virus called I Love You got into about 45 million computers.

- A real firewall keeps a building safe, while a computer firewall keeps information safe.

Safety on the Internet

As use of the Internet grows, so do problems for users. Among the worst problems are virus programs that enter your[25] computer and destroy information. Some can even destroy your computer.[35]

A *virus* can enter your computer through a virus-filled file that comes with an e-mail message. The virus can then make copies of itself and destroy what's on your computer.[66]

You can help keep information safe on your computer by taking a few steps. The first is to use a password that people[89] cannot easily guess. The second is to make sure that your computer has a firewall, a tool that keeps others out. Finally,[111] make sure you have software that can find and get rid of viruses.[124]

KEY NOTES

Safety on the Internet
Why is it important to think of safety on the Internet?

_____

_____

The Internet

History of the Internet

1. The main idea of "History of the Internet" is that _____

    a. a network of colleges runs the Internet.
    b. the Internet helps the U.S. government do its work.
    c. anyone can get on the Internet.
    d. the Internet is important to life today.

2. What is the Internet?

_____

_____

_____

3. What has happened to the Internet since 1969?

_____

_____

_____

Sending E-Mail

1. Another good name for "Sending E-mail" is _____

    a. "Packets and Headings."
    b. "How E-mail Travels."
    c. "Computers and Information."
    d. "How to Read E-mail."

2. Describe how e-mail works.

_____

_____

_____

3. How does an e-mail travel?

    a. on a path that leads to the Internet

    b. as a whole message

    c. on a special e-mail network

    d. in separate pieces of information

Buying and Selling on the Internet

1. "Buying and Selling on the Internet" is MAINLY about _____

    a. how to sell things on the Internet.

    b. how to bid on things on Web sites.

    c. how to start an Internet business.

    d. how the Internet is used for buying and selling.

2. Tell how companies have changed the way they use the Internet.

_____

_____

_____

3. Describe two ways companies and people buy and sell things on the Internet.

_____

_____

_____

Safety on the Internet

1. In this reading, *virus* means _____

    a. a germ that can make you sick.
    b. a program that can harm your computer.
    c. a program for learning new information.
    d. a copy of your e-mail messages.

2. A computer virus can _____

    a. keep your computer safe.
    b. make you sick.
    c. destroy information on your computer.
    d. protect your software with a firewall.

3. How does a computer virus work?

_____

_____

_____

Internet	computer	message	identified
purchase	company	virus	destroy

1. Choose the word from the word box above that best matches each definition. Write the word on the line below.

A. _____ to break up or tear down

B. _____ a network of computers that is linked around the world

C. _____ a group of people who work together in a business

D. _____ a machine that stores and works with information

E. _____ a program that can destroy information on a computer

F. _____ to buy something

G. _____ knew or recognized something

H. _____ a piece of information sent from one person to another

2. Fill in the blanks in the sentences below. Choose the word from the word box that completes each sentence.

A. Maria earned money so she could _____ a new backpack.

B. Ben clicked on an e-mail and soon had a _____ copying itself in his files.

C. Mrs. Santos had a _____ that sold cars.

D. Jon sent an e-mail _____ to his friend Al to tell him about the game.

E. He _____ the flower as a rose because of its color and smell.

F. Before the _____ was created, there was no e-mail.

G. The new _____ is so powerful that I can send e-mail, play games, and shop at the same time.

H. When the dog was left alone, he set out to _____ all of the pillows in the house.

75

The Internet

1. Use the idea web to help you remember what you read. In each box, write the main idea of that reading. Then, use that information to write the main idea of the topic.

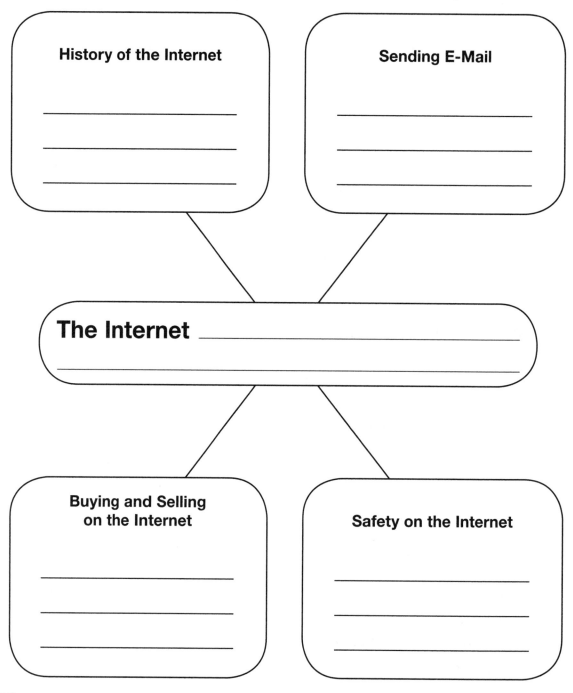

History of the Internet

Sending E-Mail

The Internet _____

Buying and Selling on the Internet

Safety on the Internet

2. How has the Internet changed the way people live today?

_____

_____

_____

_____

3. How could the Internet both bring people together and keep them apart?

_____

_____

_____

_____

4. What would you tell someone who wanted to know more about the Internet?

_____

_____

_____

_____

Creating Ads

Ads tell people to vote.

Fast Facts

- One car company spent almost $4 billion on ads in 2004.

- There are TV channels that show nothing but ads, 24 hours a day.

- More than $500 billion was spent on ads in the United States in 2004.

What's an Ad For?

Ads are everywhere, from TV to signs on cars. Most ads aim to get people to buy products and services. In our economy,[27] which is our system of making and selling goods and services, advertising helps to sell things.[43]

Ads have uses beyond just selling items. Ads tell people to vote for someone running for office. Public service ads give safety tips, such as those telling people to wear seat belts.[75]

Advertising is an important part of the economy in several ways. Advertisers pay money for time on TV. They buy space in[97] newspapers you read. Money from ads is the main way that TV and newspapers make money. Making the ads you see every day is big business, too.[124]

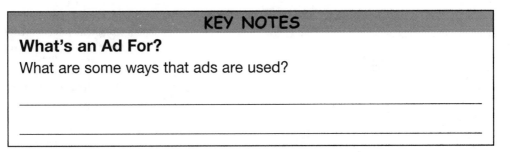

KEY NOTES

What's an Ad For?
What are some ways that ads are used?

_____

_____

Creating Ads

An ad agency starts an ad campaign for a product.

Fast Facts

- The first ad agency opened in 1843 in the United States.

- Advertisers were estimated to spend a billion dollars in 2005 a year so their products would be used on TV shows.

- Advertisers spend more than $7 billion yearly on Internet ads.

The Ad Campaign

When companies decide to advertise, they often hire an advertising agency to develop an ad campaign, a way to sell the[24] product. Developing an ad campaign is a hard job, especially today, when people get information so many ways. The agency's[44] job is to develop an ad campaign so people know about the product, talk about the product, and buy the product.[65]

The first step is to come up with an idea about the product that people will remember—and that will cause them to buy the[90] product. Then, the ad agency comes up with a plan for getting out this idea about the product. The agency may produce TV ads, newspaper ads, radio ads, and ads sent by mail.[123]

KEY NOTES

The Ad Campaign
Why does an ad campaign start with an idea about a product?

_____

_____

Creating Ads

These commercial makers are making an ad for TV.

Fast Facts

- Advertisers spend about $53 billion a year on TV ads.

- The first TV ad was made in 1941 for a watch company and cost $9.

- A half-hour TV show has eight minutes of ads.

Making TV Commercials

Making TV ads, or commercials, is part of the film business. People who make TV commercials often go through the same[24] steps that people who make movies do. The difference is that moviemakers want to entertain you. The people who make TV[45] commercials are more interested in making you buy than in entertaining you.[57]

First, the commercial makers come up with a story for the spot, as TV commercials are called. Then, actors try out and[79] are hired. If the product is for young people, the actors may be young people. If the product is for older people, the actors[103] will likely be older. The idea is that if people your age buy the product, you might want to, too.[123]

KEY NOTES

Making TV Commercials
What is the difference between movies and commercials?

_____

_____

Creating Ads

Posters are one type of print ad.

Fast Facts

- Advertisers spent more than $21 billion on magazine ads in 2004.

- Ads appeared in ancient Rome, where people wrote them on walls.

- Ads began to appear in English newspapers in the seventeenth century.

Making Print Ads

An ad campaign often has ads that appear in several places. Usually, print ads are part of a campaign. Print ads are ads[26] in newspapers and magazines. A campaign may also run ads on billboards. These different ways of advertising help reach different people.[47]

Often, an ad campaign will make sure the ads it runs all look similar, so a magazine ad will have the same theme as[71] the TV ads. These ads use the same actors and same taglines, or sayings about the product. Instead of being said by actors,[94] though, these taglines are written into the ads. The different ways of presenting the same theme helps the readers or[114] viewers remember the ad—and, more important, remember the product.[124]

KEY NOTES

Making Print Ads
Why do ad campaigns have TV and print ads?

_____

_____

Creating Ads

What's an Ad For?

1. Another good name for "What's an Ad For?" is _____

    a. "Public Service Ads."
    b. "Ads on TV."
    c. "Why Ads Are Everywhere."
    d. "Selling Products."

2. Why is there so much advertising?

_____

_____

_____

3. Why are ads an important part of the economy?

_____

_____

_____

The Ad Campaign

1. What is an ad campaign?

_____

_____

_____

2. What is the main job of an ad agency?

    a. to develop products
    b. to develop an ad campaign
    c. to talk about products
    d. to produce TV shows with ads

3. What steps does an ad agency take to make an ad campaign?

_____

_____

_____

Making TV Commercials

1. What is the main idea of "Making TV Commercials"?

    a. Anyone can make TV commercials.
    b. TV commercials are made to get people to buy.
    c. TV shows sell products.
    d. People in ads are young.

2. How are commercials like full-length films?

    a. Both are made through the same kinds of steps.
    b. Both are the same length.
    c. Both are made to sell products.
    d. Both are made mostly for young people.

3. Why do advertisers put young people in commercials for certain products?

_____

_____

_____

Making Print Ads

1. "Making Print Ads" is MAINLY about how _____

    a. print ads run on TV.

    b. print ads are often part of a larger ad campaign.

    c. print ads have different themes than TV ads do.

    d. print ads use actors.

2. Why would an ad campaign use print ads?

_____

_____

_____

3. Ads for an ad campaign have the same theme so people _____

    a. know where to find the ads.

    b. see lots of ads.

    c. read the same newspaper every day.

    d. will remember the ad and the product.

advertising	economy	agency	campaign
commercial	entertain	magazine	theme

1. Choose the word from the word box above that best matches each definition. Write the word on the line below.

A. _____ to keep interested

B. _____ an idea that is central

C. _____ a paid advertisement on TV

D. _____ written or spoken matter that tells about a product

E. _____ a system of buying and selling goods and services

F. _____ reading matter that is printed usually weekly or monthly

G. _____ a set of actions or ideas developed to get something done

H. _____ an office or business

2. Fill in the blanks in the sentences below. Choose the word from the word box that completes each sentence.

A. In our _____, people produce, sell, and buy things.

B. That _____ about sports comes out every month.

C. The _____ that wrote the ads also made the TV spots.

D. The ad _____ had TV ads and print ads.

E. Did you see that the newspaper is full of _____ today?

F. Darcy wanted to have a holiday _____ for our party.

G. We hired clowns to _____ the children.

H. That TV _____ cow made me laugh.

Creating Ads

1. Use the idea web to help you remember what you read. In each box, write the main idea of that reading.

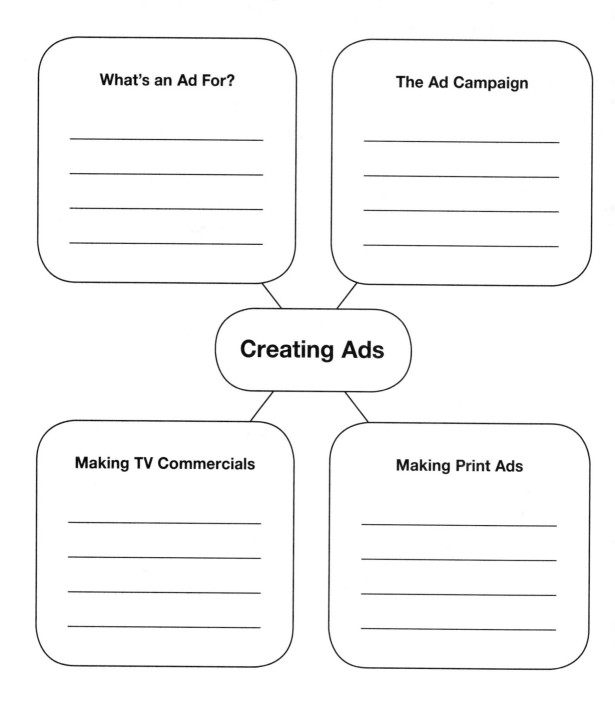

What's an Ad For?

_____

_____

_____

_____

The Ad Campaign

_____

_____

_____

_____

Creating Ads

Making TV Commercials

_____

_____

_____

_____

Making Print Ads

_____

_____

_____

_____

2. How are print and TV ads alike and different?

_____

_____

_____

_____

3. Tell two things you learned about making advertisements from these readings.

_____

_____

_____

_____

4. Think of an ad campaign you think works and tell why you think that.

_____

_____

_____

_____

Taking Care of the Human Body

The human body is very complex.

Fast Facts

- Goosebumps happen when pores in the skin close to keep heat inside the body.

- The surface area of the lungs is about the size of a tennis court.

- The human body has about 100 trillion cells.

The Systems of the Human Body

People use some tools and machines, such as pens, that are simple. Other tools, such as cars, are complex. However, no machine is as complex as the human body.[35]

Inside your body are systems that do special jobs. The job of one system is to keep you breathing. Another system's job[57] involves moving blood throughout your body. In all, ten different systems keep your body going. All of these systems are inside[78] your body except one. That system covers all the other systems. It is your skin.[93]

To keep your body working well, you need to take care of it. This care involves everything from taking care that the outside[116] is clean to making sure the systems inside are kept strong with a healthful diet and exercise.[133]

KEY NOTES

The Systems of the Human Body

How is the human body like a machine?

_____

_____

Taking Care of the Human Body

This drawing shows how blood circulates by traveling through veins and arteries.

Fast Facts

- The heart beats about 100,000 times a day.

- An adult's heart is about the size of two fists.

- In a day, your blood travels about 12,000 miles.

The Circulatory System

The tiny blue lines that you see through your skin are part of your body's circulatory system. The circulatory system's job is to circulate blood throughout your body.[31]

Your veins and arteries are the tubes that carry blood around your body. Red blood that is rich in oxygen runs through[53] the arteries to all parts of the body. Veins carry blood back to the heart. The blood in the veins looks blue because some of[78] the oxygen is gone. Once the heart and lungs put oxygen back into the blood, the blood is ready to circulate through the body again.[103]

One way to stay healthy is to exercise about a half-hour most days of the week. Exercise keeps your circulatory system, and the rest of your body, in shape.[133]

KEY NOTES

The Circulatory System
What is the circulatory system?

_____

_____

Taking Care of the Human Body

Keeping germs out helps the body repair itself.

Fast Facts

- The skin is the largest organ in the body.

- Hairs in the nose help clean the air you breathe.

- People shed about 40 pounds of skin in their lifetime.

The Body's Repair Kit

The human body is designed to keep germs out. Skin forms a protective covering over the systems inside the body. Where[25] there are openings in the skin, the body has ways to protect itself. For example, lids and lashes keep the eyes clean. Both[48] hairs in the nose and wax in the ears catch germs that could cause illness.[63]

When germs do get in, the human body uses its own repair kit. White blood cells protect the body by killing harmful germs.[86] The body also repairs cuts. Blood dries and forms a clot, or scab, over a cut. New skin grows under the scab, repairing the cut.[111] You can help your body repair cuts by keeping cuts clean and covered until your body has a chance to repair itself.[133]

KEY NOTES

The Body's Repair Kit

What is in the body's repair kit?

_____

_____

Taking Care of the Human Body

Exercise makes the body stronger.

Fast Facts

- Muscles don't grow during exercise. They grow afterward, when people rest.

- People can lose a quart of water an hour by sweating.

- An adult's body has about 10 gallons of water.

Keeping the Body Going

The human body can repair itself, but it does need help from its owner. One thing people need to stay healthy is the[27] right food. Eating the right combination of foods gives people the energy they need to learn, work, and grow. Because more[48] than half of the body is water, people need to restore their body's water supply by drinking plenty of water.[68]

The human body also needs sleep and exercise. The body's systems restore their energy during sleep. Exercise makes the[87] heart and lungs strong. Strong hearts and lungs get energy and oxygen to the muscles quickly. Some ways to make your heart[109] and lungs stronger are by riding a bike, dancing, walking, and swimming. A combination of different types of exercise will help even more.[132]

KEY NOTES

Keeping the Body Going
What kind of help does the body need to stay healthy?

_____

_____

Taking Care of the Human Body

The Systems of the Human Body

1. "The Systems of the Human Body" is MAINLY about _____

    a. the hidden systems of the body.
    b. the systems that help the human body work.
    c. how to use simple and complex machines.
    d. the systems of all living things.

2. What are three jobs that the human body's systems do?

_____

_____

_____

3. What are two ways people can take care of their body?

_____

_____

_____

The Circulatory System

1. Which of the following are part of the circulatory system?

    a. veins and arteries
    b. skin and veins
    c. oxygen and blood
    d. the body's tubes and skin

2. What does the circulatory system do?

_____

_____

_____

3. What is one way to keep your circulatory system in shape?

_____

_____

_____

The Body's Repair Kit

1. How does the body protect itself?

    a. with the circulatory system
    b. by using protective coverings on the skin
    c. by keeping germs out
    d. with openings in the skin, nose, and ears

2. How does the body repair itself?

    a. with white blood cells
    b. by forming germs
    c. with eyelids and eyelashes
    d. by keeping cuts clean and covered

3. How can you help your body heal itself?

_____

_____

_____

Keeping the Body Going

1. The main idea of "Keeping the Body Going" is that _____

    a. people need to eat the right foods.
    b. people need to sleep and exercise.
    c. people can make their hearts stronger.
    d. people can help their body stay healthy.

2. People can make their heart and lungs stronger by _____

    a. drinking plenty of water.
    b. breathing slowly.
    c. building the white blood cells.
    d. getting enough sleep and exercise.

3. What are three things people can do to keep their body going?

_____

_____

_____

complex	involve	veins	arteries	circulatory
protective	repair	restore	combination	

1. Choose the word from the word box above that best matches each definition. Write the word on the line below.

A. _____ to fix something

B. _____ tubes that take blood to the heart

C. _____ keeping safe from harm

D. _____ a mixture of things

E. _____ having many connected parts

F. _____ to bring something back to good condition

G. _____ tubes that take blood from the heart to the body

H. _____ to include

I. _____ relating to the system that includes the heart and the blood

2. Fill in the blanks in the sentences below. Choose the word from the word box that completes each sentence.

A. The car is broken, so we have to _____ it.

B. Because it has many parts, a computer is a _____ machine.

C. His _____ looked blue because the blood in them had little oxygen.

D. Those flowers contain a _____ of tulips and roses.

E. In the _____ system, the heart and lungs get oxygen to the body's cells.

F. The _____ carry blood from the heart to the rest of the body.

G. I will _____ myself with the food bank to help hungry people.

H. Skin is a _____ organ because it keeps body systems safe.

I. The city will _____ the park so people can use it again.

103

Taking Care of the Human Body

1. Use the idea web to help you remember what you read. In each box, write the main idea of that reading. Then, use that information to write the main idea of the topic.

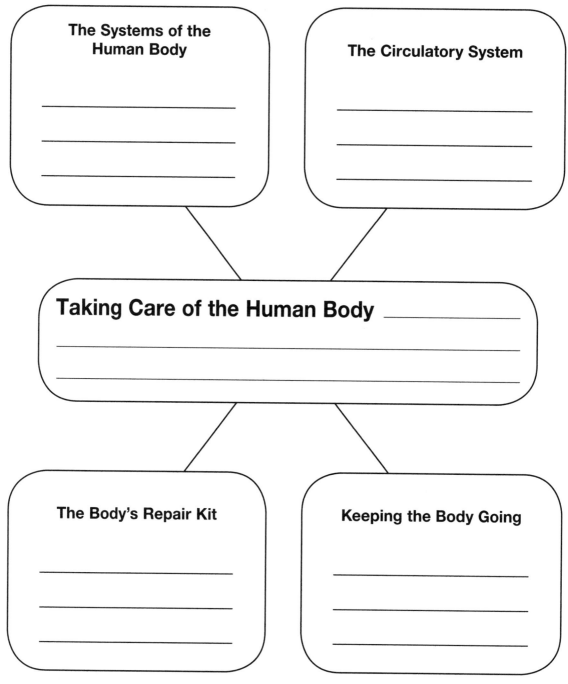

The Systems of the Human Body

_____

_____

_____

The Circulatory System

_____

_____

_____

Taking Care of the Human Body _____

_____

_____

The Body's Repair Kit

_____

_____

_____

Keeping the Body Going

_____

_____

_____

2. Why is the human body called a complex machine?

_____

_____

_____

_____

3. Describe two systems that are working in your body now.

_____

_____

_____

_____

4. How can you help two of your body's systems work better?

_____

_____

_____

_____

Volcanoes

This active volcano in Washington State erupted in 1980.

Fast Facts

- The 1980 volcanic eruption in Washington State killed 24,000 animals.

- An 1815 volcanic eruption in Asia killed 92,000 people.

- Rocks and ash can travel 250 miles per hour in a volcanic eruption.

Kinds of Volcanoes

The word *volcano* probably makes you think of red-hot lava erupting from a mountain. This idea is correct, at least[24] while the volcano erupts. However, many volcanoes are extinct. An extinct, or dead, volcano will never erupt again.[42]

Active volcanoes are volcanoes that might erupt again. The world has more than 1,500 active volcanoes. Some[59] active volcanoes are quiet for hundreds of years before they erupt again.[71]

Some volcanoes have small eruptions. Others explode with great force. Scientists who study volcanoes can usually[87] tell when a volcano will erupt. Sometimes, though, volcanoes can surprise even scientists. Scientists thought a volcano[104] might erupt at some time in Washington State. However, in 1980, when it did erupt, 57 people died and large areas of the state were covered with volcanic ash.[133]

KEY NOTES

Kinds of Volcanoes
What are two kinds of volcanoes?

_____

_____

Volcanoes

This drawing shows plates of the Earth's crust.

Fast Facts

- Some scientists think a huge volcanic eruption killed the dinosaurs.

- Volcanoes can send ash 10,000 feet into the air.

- The tallest volcano in the world is more than 6 miles high.

How Volcanoes Form

A volcano is an opening in the crust, or outside layer, of Earth. The opening leads to a deeper layer of Earth called the[27] mantle. Think of Earth as a peach. The skin would be Earth's crust and the juicy part would be Earth's mantle. Earth's mantle is made of white-hot rock called magma.[58]

Earth's crust is broken into pieces called plates. When plates separate, a crack opens and magma escapes as lava.[77] Layers of lava form the volcano's cone. Then, the volcano erupts, sending lava and ash onto the land.[95]

Volcanoes also form when plates move together and overlap. The bottom plate sinks into Earth's mantle. Rock from the[114] sinking plate melts into magma that is forced to the surface. That melted rock can then erupt from the volcano.[134]

KEY NOTES

How Volcanoes Form
How does a volcano's cone form?

_____

_____

Volcanoes

Magma, or lava, erupts from a volcano.

Fast Facts

- In Africa, the poisonous gases from a 1986 volcanic eruption killed 1,700 people.

- Ash from a volcano can cause roofs to fall and crops to fail.

- Volcanic ash can make soil better for growing crops.

When Volcanoes Erupt

A volcanic eruption happens when magma is forced up through a volcano. The magma that erupts from volcanoes[21] is called lava. Lava can reach a temperature of 2,000 degrees Fahrenheit. A temperature of 2,000 degrees Fahrenheit is[40] almost four times hotter than the hottest setting of an oven. As lava flows, it burns the plants and trees in its path. Even[64] trees that are miles away can die because the heat from the eruption dries out their sap.[81]

Clouds of hot, poisonous gases from inside Earth also escape when a volcano erupts. These poisonous gases are dangerous to[101] breathe. An eruption's blast shatters cooled lava into tiny bits of ash. Volcanic ash can fall like snow for miles around. Other lava that cools quickly becomes black, shiny rock.[131]

KEY NOTES

When Volcanoes Erupt
What happens when volcanoes erupt?

_____

_____

Volcanoes

Lava in Hawaii flows into the ocean, building up more rock.

Peter French / PacificStock.com

Fast Facts

- A volcanic eruption destroyed an island in Asia in 1883.

- Hawaii is made up of 132 islands and reefs.

- The oldest Hawaiian island was formed about 5 million years ago.

Volcanic Islands

The islands of Hawaii were formed by volcanoes that erupted from a hot spot in Earth's mantle. Hot spots are places[23] where huge amounts of magma build up in Earth's mantle and often erupt. Where Hawaii is now, ancient eruptions of[43] lava flowed onto the ocean floor and cooled to become hard rock. Later eruptions spilled new lava, and, as the process was repeated, the pile of rock grew.[71]

With each new eruption, the pile of cooled lava grew higher. When the cooled lava reached the ocean's surface, an island[92] formed. As the plate moved above the hot spot, a new volcano formed and another island began. By repeating this process,[113] the hot spot slowly built a chain of islands. The state of Hawaii is made up of islands like these.[133]

KEY NOTES

Volcanic Islands

How were the islands of Hawaii formed?

_____

_____

Volcanoes

Kinds of Volcanoes

1. Another good name for "Kinds of Volcanoes" is _____

  a. "Active and Extinct Volcanoes."
  b. "When Volcanoes Erupt."
  c. "How Volcanoes Behave."
  d. "Scientists Who Were Surprised by Volcanoes."

2. What are active volcanoes?

_____

_____

_____

3. What are extinct volcanoes?

_____

_____

_____

How Volcanoes Form

1. How do volcanoes form?

  a. Two of Earth's plates make a new mantle.
  b. Earth's crust is broken into pieces.
  c. Earth's mantle flows into volcanic magma.
  d. Lava escapes through Earth's crust.

2. The mantle of Earth is _____

    a. the plates of the Earth.
    b. Earth's crust.
    c. a deep layer of Earth.
    d. an opening in Earth.

3. What are two ways volcanoes form?

_____

_____

_____

When Volcanoes Erupt

1. Why are volcanoes dangerous?

    a. Earth can lose its lava when volcanoes erupt.
    b. Ash and hot gases can cause cracks to form in Earth's crust.
    c. Hot lava and poisonous gases can hurt living things.
    d. Hot lava can heat up the magma inside Earth.

2. A volcanic eruption happens when _____

    a. magma is forced up through a volcano.
    b. lava is melted by the Sun.
    c. poisonous gases escape from Earth.
    d. Earth's temperature rises.

3. What are two things that can come from Earth when a volcano erupts?

_____

_____

_____

Volcanic Islands

1. "Volcanic Islands" is MAINLY about _____

a. how all islands are formed by volcanoes.
b. how lava erupts inside the volcanoes of Hawaii.
c. how the islands of Hawaii were formed.
d. how volcanoes made hot spots in Hawaii.

2. What is a hot spot?

_____

_____

_____

3. How do volcanoes form an island?

_____

_____

_____

volcano	erupt	extinct	mantle	magma
Fahrenheit	poisonous	Hawaii	repeated	

1. Choose the word from the word box above that best matches each definition. Write the word on the line below.

A. _____ able to kill or hurt

B. _____ a scale that measures temperature

C. _____ done again and again

D. _____ an opening in Earth's surface that sometimes throws out lava, ash, and hot gas

E. _____ to break out, like an explosion

F. _____ a layer of Earth below the crust

G. _____ the islands that form the fiftieth state of the United States

H. _____ rock that is melted deep inside Earth

I. _____ no longer alive

2. Fill in the blanks in the sentences below. Choose the word from the word box that completes each sentence.

A. When volcanoes _____, they can kill all of the living things nearby.

B. When _____ comes to the surface, it becomes lava.

C. Because it is made from islands, the state of _____ has many beaches.

D. That mushroom is _____, so don't eat it.

E. Plants and animals become _____ when the last one dies.

F. The temperature is 40 degrees _____, so you need a coat.

G. That _____ could erupt at any time.

H. Below Earth's crust is a layer called the _____.

I. He _____ that song so many times we got tired of hearing it.

Volcanoes

1. Use the idea web to help you remember what you read. In each box, write the main idea of that reading.

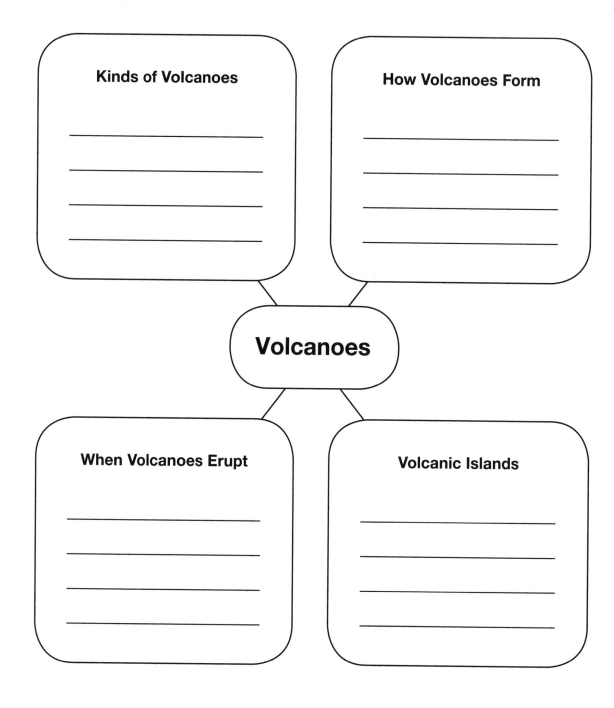

Kinds of Volcanoes

_____

_____

_____

_____

How Volcanoes Form

_____

_____

_____

Volcanoes

When Volcanoes Erupt

_____

_____

_____

_____

Volcanic Islands

_____

_____

_____

_____

2. What are three facts you learned about volcanoes?

_____

_____

_____

_____

3. How might Earth be different if there were no volcanoes?

_____

_____

_____

_____

4. Name one good thing and one bad thing that can happen when a volcano erupts.

_____

_____

_____

_____

Wind and Solar Energy

This wind turbine and generator will never run out of fuel—the wind.

Fast Facts

- The fastest recorded wind gust was 231 miles per hour.

- On the planet Neptune, the winds blow at 900 miles per hour.

- The South Pole is the windiest place on Earth.

Wind Energy

For thousands of years, people used energy from the Sun and the wind to keep them warm and help them work. Today,[24] we get much of the energy we use from coal, oil, and gas. However, these fuels cannot be replaced once they run out.[47]

To meet our future needs, scientists are exploring how people once used energy from the Sun and the wind. They hope[68] to use these ideas again and to develop new ways to use these endless sources of energy.[85]

Wind energy is created when wind blows through turbines. A turbine is like a reverse fan. In a wind turbine, the wind[107] turns the blades that turn the generator. The generator in the wind turbine then produces electricity. Because wind is always being replaced, wind energy cannot run out.[134]

KEY NOTES

Wind Energy
How can wind make energy?

_____

_____

Wind and Solar Energy

Turbines on a wind farm turn many generators, which create electricity.

Fast Facts

- Windmills, which were used to pump water, were an early way to use wind energy.

- As much as one-quarter of the United States may have winds strong enough to produce electricity.

- The blades of the largest wind turbine span the length of a football field.

Wind Farms

A wind farm is made up of turbines that turn wind energy into electricity. Wind farms need strong, steady winds, so they [24] are built where the usual wind speed is at least 13 miles per hour. Without wind, turbines cannot produce electricity. [44]

In California, a wind farm with 7,000 turbines was built in a mountain pass that has strong summer winds. This California [65] wind farm generates the electricity needed to run fans and other cooling systems. [78]

Electricity from wind farms is cheaper today than it was 10 years ago. In addition, wind energy does not produce gases [99] that pollute the air. Even so, some people don't like wind farms. They say wind farms take up too much land, pollute the air with noise, and spoil the beauty of the landscape. [132]

KEY NOTES

Wind Farms

Where are wind farms built?

_____

_____

Wind and Solar Energy

Solar panels on this roof in Hawaii receive direct sunlight.

Carl Shaneff / PacificStock.com

Fast Facts

- Some homes are heated by solar cells on their roof.

- Solar systems power some traffic lights.

- At its core, the Sun can reach 27 million degrees Fahrenheit.

Solar Energy

The Sun has an endless supply of energy. A few minutes
of the Sun's light could run all the machines in the world for[26]
a year. To be used as electricity, however, the Sun's energy, or
solar energy, must be stored.[43]

A house that receives direct sunlight will be warmer at
night because the Sun was shining on it. Solar energy warmed[64]
the house. A toaster or TV won't work in the same way, though.
These machines cannot use solar energy directly.[84]

Solar cells can change solar energy into electricity.
Many calculators run on solar cells. However, although many[101]
calculators and other machines use solar cells, solar power is
not a major power source today. Scientists are still looking for
better and cheaper ways to store the Sun's energy.[131]

KEY NOTES

Solar Energy
How can solar energy be used?

_____

_____

Wind and Solar Energy

Solar energy runs this car.

Fast Facts

- Experimental solar cars can cost more than $1 million.

- Solar cars can go 100 miles per hour.

- A solar car can weigh 800 pounds, whereas most regular cars weigh about 3,000 pounds.

Solar Cars

In the year 2000, a solar-powered car traveled 4,400 miles and set a distance record. The car was tiny and light and held[26] only one person. Its source, or energy, was the solar cells on its roof.[40]

To go that distance, the car used about the same amount of energy as a toaster. On cloudy or rainy days, the car used[64] solar energy stored in a battery. When the battery power ran out, the car couldn't move until the Sun shone, restarting the solar cells and storing energy in the battery.[94]

This example shows that while solar cells may someday be a common energy source, they are not yet ready for everyday[115] use. Scientists keep working on solar cars, though, because they use less energy and do not pollute the air.[134]

KEY NOTES

Solar Cars
How do solar cars work?

_____

_____

Wind and Solar Energy

Wind Energy

1. Long ago, what did people use for energy?

a. the wind and the Sun
b. coal and gas
c. electricity and the wind
d. oil and generators

2. How does a wind turbine produce electricity?

_____

_____

_____

3. Name two energy sources that can run out and two that cannot.

_____

_____

_____

Wind Farms

1. What is a wind farm?

a. a field of wind turbines
b. a farm that gets too much wind
c. a place where wind is made
d. a farm where the air is polluted

2. The main idea of "Wind Farms" is that _____

    a. wind farms make the wind that turns turbines.
    b. the wind is strong in California.
    c. turbines make wind power.
    d. windy places can be used to make electricity.

3. Give two reasons people like wind farms and two reasons they do not.

_____

_____

_____

Solar Energy

1. Another good name for "Solar Energy" is _____

    a. "A New Form of Energy."
    b. "Turning Sunshine Into Electricity."
    c. "Better Ways to Power Calculators."
    d. "The History of Solar Energy."

2. How do solar cells work?

    a. They store the energy made on summer days.
    b. They run machines at night.
    c. They change solar energy into electricity.
    d. They give off sunlight when it's dark.

3. Why is solar power not a major power source today?

_____

_____

_____

Solar Cars

_____

_____

_____

2. Which of these is a fact about the solar-powered car that went 4,400 miles?

    a. The car used gas on cloudy or rainy days.

    b. The car was too heavy to go very far.

    c. The car couldn't run when the battery power ran out.

    d. The car needed wind power and solar power to move.

3. Why are scientists interested in making solar cars?

_____

_____

_____

turbine	generator	California	pollute
solar	calculators	distance	battery

1. Choose the word from the word box above that best matches each definition. Write the word on the line below.

A. _____ having to do with the Sun

B. _____ a large state on the west coast of the United States

C. _____ tools for doing math

D. _____ the amount of space between two points

E. _____ a machine that turns and makes power

F. _____ to make something dirty

G. _____ a machine that can make electricity

H. _____ a cell that can store electricity

2. Fill in the blanks in the sentences below. Choose the word from the word box that completes each sentence.

A. We need to put in a new _____ so we can use the phone.

B. That area is windy, so it is a good place to make energy with a wind _____.

C. Jim picked up the trash because he didn't want to _____ the ground.

D. The large state on the west coast of the United States is _____.

E. The _____ runs on gas, so we can have light even if the electricity goes off.

F. The class was allowed to use _____ on the final exam.

G. _____ energy doesn't work well on cloudy days.

H. The _____ from my home to the mall is about 2 miles.

Wind and Solar Energy

1. Use the Venn diagram to help you remember what you read. In the center area, write how the two kinds of energy are similar. In the outside areas, write how they are different from each other.

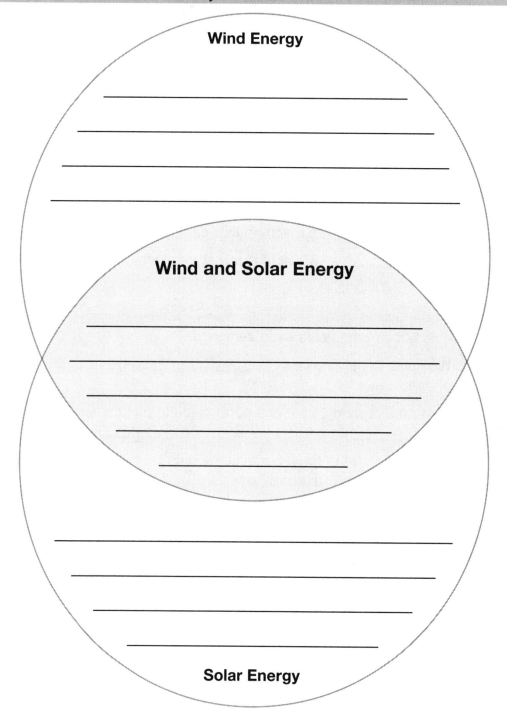

Wind Energy

_____

_____

_____

_____

Wind and Solar Energy

_____

_____

_____

_____

_____

_____

_____

_____

_____

Solar Energy

2. Name two reasons people want to get energy from the wind and the Sun.

_____

_____

_____

_____

3. Name two reasons why wind power and solar power are not used more widely.

_____

_____

_____

_____

4. How would the world be different if wind and solar power were used more often?

_____

_____

_____

_____

The Origins of Sports

A streetball tournament in New York City happens every year.

Fast Facts

- The streetball tournament is still a big event in New York City.

- A TV show was made about streetball.

- Many pro basketball stars started in streetball.

Streetball

It was 1946 and another hot summer in New York City. That summer, a worker for the city began a street basketball[23] tournament. That tournament was the origin of a sport that many people play today. Streetball, as it is called, is like basketball,[45] but it is different, too, because the origins of streetball are in the street, not the gym.[62]

Streetball is fast, and style counts more than it does in basketball. There is no net because most baskets have no nets.[84] In streetball, a group of people decide the rules and play. Most streetball is played without refs.[101]

Like many games, streetball comes from a particular place. Streetball was born because New York City had basketball[119] hoops and hard surfaces on which to bounce basketballs. New York City still has these, and streetball is still played off and on its streets.[144]

KEY NOTES

Streetball
What is streetball?

_____

_____

The Origins of Sports

Snowboarders use their arms for balance.

Fast Facts

- In 1998, snowboarding became a sport at the Olympic Games.

- The first snowboard was called a Snurfer.

- In 1982, the first national snowboard race was held in Vermont.

Snowboarding

In the snowy hills of Michigan in 1965, a father made a toy
for his daughter. He put together two skis with a rope at the [27]
tip so the rider could hold the toy as it went down hills. His
daughter's friends loved it, so the Michigan man made more.
By 1966, more than half a million of these toys were sold. [63]

The new sport got the name snowboarding, and soon many
people were making snowboards. One was a young man who [83]
rode trays down the hills at his school. The young man started
a business called Winterstick to make his snowboards. Unlike [104]
the ones first made in Michigan, these snowboards did not have
a rope. Instead, snowboarders used their arms for balance. [124]

The sport has grown. At first, many ski areas did not allow
snowboarders, but now almost all do. [142]

KEY NOTES

Snowboarding
What is snowboarding?

_____

_____

The Origins of Sports

Rhymes and two twirling ropes are part of double Dutch jump rope.

Fast Facts

- The first jump ropes may have come from ancient China.

- The first double Dutch meet, which was held in New York in 1974, had nearly 600 jumpers.

- Today, double Dutch meets attract about 100,000 people from around the world.

Double Dutch Jump Rope

Jump rope made its way across the ocean with Europeans who settled on the east coast of North America. Although many[25] children in Europe jumped rope, Dutch children played the game in a different way.[39]

Two children held the ends of two ropes and turned them in different directions. Another child stood within the twirling[59] ropes, jumping over and under them. When English children saw jump rope played this way, they named it double Dutch.[79]

The game was always common in New York City, but in the mid-20th century, a double Dutch craze began. Children[100] said rhymes as they jumped to the difficult beat of the twirling ropes.[113]

In the 1970s, the game became a sport, with teams saying rhymes as they competed to show their speed and skill. Today, double Dutch jumpers compete in meets around the world.[144]

KEY NOTES

Double Dutch Jump Rope   How is double Dutch jump rope different from other kinds of rope jumping?

_____

_____

The Origins of Sports

Stock cars are built to race on a track.

Fast Facts

- Prize money for a NASCAR race can be more than $10 million.

- A NASCAR team with one car can cost as much as $20 million a year.

- After football, NASCAR has the most fans of any sport in the United States.

Stock Car Racing

When World War II ended, U.S. carmakers turned their attention from tanks to cars. They made fast, powerful cars, and young men loved racing them.[28]

People in different parts of the country raced different kinds of cars. In the South, people raced stock cars—cars from a car[51] dealer. In 1948, a racer named Bill France organized stock car racers into an association called the National Association for[71] Stock Car Auto Racing, or NASCAR. Members raced stock cars on oval tracks.[84]

From the time it was organized, NASCAR grew into a huge sport and a big business. Today, even though almost all the[106] drivers and teams are in the South, millions of fans around the country watch NASCAR drivers race. These cars don't come[127] from the dealer anymore. Instead, they're designed for one thing—going as fast as possible.[142]

KEY NOTES

Stock Car Racing
What is stock car racing?

_____

_____

The Origins of Sports

Streetball

1. The main idea of "Streetball" is that streetball _____

    a. is a kind of basketball.
    b. can be played in streets or in fields.
    c. is played in gyms.
    d. is a kind of football.

2. Tell three ways streetball is different from basketball.

_____

_____

_____

3. Tell how streetball began.

_____

_____

_____

Snowboarding

1. The first snowboard might have been made in Michigan because

_____

    a. people in Michigan like surfing.
    b. winters are sunny and warm in Michigan.
    c. Michigan is hilly and snowy.
    d. people in Michigan make a lot of toys.

2. What is a snowboard?

_____

_____

_____

3. How have snowboards changed?

    a. Now, they have ropes.

    b. They were first used all year.

    c. Now, they don't have ropes.

    d. They cannot be used in ski areas.

Double Dutch Jump Rope

1. Another good name for "Double Dutch Jump Rope" is _____

    a. "How to Jump Rope."

    b. "Buying Jump Ropes."

    c. "Games of Early Settlers."

    d. "Jump Rope Becomes a Sport."

2. What is double Dutch jump rope?

_____

_____

_____

3. How did double Dutch jump rope become a sport?

_____

_____

_____

Stock Car Racing

"Stock Car Racing" is MAINLY about _____

    a. how stock cars work.

    b. what stock cars are.

    c. the history of stock car racing.

    d. how to race a stock car.

2. What is NASCAR?

_____

_____

_____

3. Stock car racing began _____

    a. when soldiers raced in World War II.

    b. when U.S. carmakers made fast cars.

    c. when soldiers bought cars.

    d. when U.S. carmakers began racing cars.

tournament	origin	Michigan	daughter
double	rhymes	organized	association

1. Choose the word from the word box above that best matches each definition. Write the word on the line below.

A. _____ a series of contests in which people or teams of people take part

B. _____ words that have the same sounds at the ends

C. _____ a female child

D. _____ having two parts that are alike

E. _____ beginnings

F. _____ put together or arranged in a certain way

G. _____ groups or people joined together for a purpose

H. _____ a midwestern U.S. state

2. Fill in the blanks in the sentences below. Choose the word from the word box that completes each sentence.

A. We joined the car racing _____ because we liked to watch fast cars.

B. Our town had twice as many people as before, so we needed to _____ the number of schools.

C. Ralph has two sons and one _____.

D. *At*, *cat*, and *hat* are all _____.

E. There's a lot of snow in _____ in the winter.

F. Our team will compete in the basketball _____.

G. No one knows the _____ of some sports because they've been played for many years.

H. She _____ the first bird-watching club in the area.

The Origins of Sports

1. Use the chart to help you remember what you read. In each box, write what you learned about each sport in this topic.

STREETBALL

Where It Began	How You Play It

SNOWBOARDING

Where It Began	How You Play It

DOUBLE DUTCH JUMP ROPE

Where It Began	How You Play It

STOCK CAR RACING

Where It Began	How You Play It

2. What two sports that you read about became popular in
New York City?

_____

_____

_____

_____

3. Why do you think two of the sports you read about started where
they did?

_____

_____

_____

_____

4. Compare two of the sports you read about.

_____

_____

_____

_____

Art and Technology

A car designer creates cars by using computer-aided design (CAD).

Fast Facts

- An idea for modern computers dates from the 1830s.

- In 1857, Leon Scott invented a way to record sound.

- By the 1960s, artists were using computers to create art and music.

Technology Changes the Arts

New technologies, or new ways of doing things, have changed the world. Today, we can ride in planes instead of[24] riding on horses. That's because of new technology. We can send mail through computers instead of through the post office.[44] New technologies have changed art and music, too. Although artists still use paint and musicians still play pianos, new[63] technologies allow artists and musicians to create their work in new ways.[75]

Perhaps the most exciting part of these new technologies is that they have created new ways to create art works. Just as[97] people still send letters through the post office, people still use paint and pianos without speakers. Today, however, artists[116] can paint with beams of light. Musicians can write music with computers. Technology adds richness to the ways people can create and experience the arts.[141]

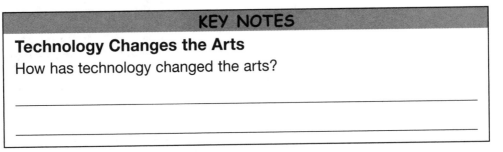

KEY NOTES
Technology Changes the Arts
How has technology changed the arts?

Art and Technology

Digital cameras can load images onto computers.

Fast Facts

- The first photograph of nature was taken in 1826.

- The first color photo was taken in 1861.

- When the first photographs were taken, people had to stay still for minutes while the camera recorded the picture.

Digital Photography

At first, many people thought that photography was not really one of the arts. A photograph, after all, was nothing[22] more than a picture of something that existed in life. Early in the 20th century, though, people began to think of[43] photographs as art. They understood that photographers chose their subjects and arranged them just as painters did. Today, photography is an accepted art form.[67]

Although photography was once a new technology, digital photography has become an even newer technology.[82] Digital cameras store photos on memory chips, not on film. Photographers using this new technology do not need a[101] darkroom. Instead, they load their images on a computer and print them on a printer. Artists can easily change the colors,[122] sizes, and shapes of their subjects on a computer screen. Digital photographers can also create photographs that look like paintings.[142]

KEY NOTES

Digital Photography
What is digital photography?

_____

_____

Art and Technology

Synthesizers can sound like the piano and other instruments.

Fast Facts

- The music synthesizer was invented in 1955.

- The first synthesizer was the size of a room.

- Composers who once needed a large group of musicians to play their work now can hear it on a single computer.

Music and Computers

At first, people did not think computers should be used in music. Some people wondered if musicians were really[22] composing music if they used a computer. If the sounds weren't coming from instruments, were they listening to real music?[42]

There are several ways musicians can use computers as they write and perform. Composers can program a computer[60] with sounds and rhythms and tell the computer how to arrange them. Composers can also tell a computer to add sounds that[82] no instrument can make. The work can then be played either by instruments or on a machine called a synthesizer.[102] A synthesizer has a keyboard and can make the sounds of other instruments.[115]

Musicians can also use a computer to write music. They play a song, and the computer records the sounds and turns them into written music that others can play.[144]

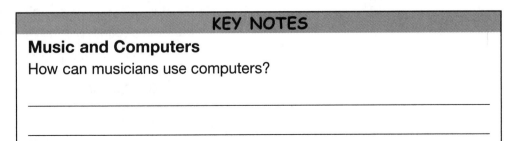

KEY NOTES

Music and Computers
How can musicians use computers?

_____

_____

Art and Technology

Some artists are digital painters.

Fast Facts

- A company offering computer art greeting cards online was sold for $780 million.

- The first computer art competition was held in 1963.

- One piece of computer-generated artwork is a wall-sized head that answers questions people ask it.

Computer Art

Artists began using computers to create art in the early 1960s. As with music, some people did not think that art and[24] computers should be used together. Computer artists, though, proved that computers could be used as an artist's tool.[42]

Some techniques allow artists to create and change images on a computer screen. One technique, called digital[59] painting, is like painting or drawing that is done on a computer screen, not on paper. Digital painters draw with a[80] stylus, or a special pen, on a tablet that is connected to the computer. The lines drawn by the stylus then appear on the[104] computer screen. Using this technique, painters can work on one part of a painting and easily transfer their work to[124] another part of the painting. Later, they can print their work and hang it on a wall.[141]

KEY NOTES

Computer Art

How can computers be used in art?

_____

_____

Art and Technology

Technology Changes the Arts

1. The main idea of "Technology Changes the Arts" is that _____

    a. art today is always made with technology.
    b. technology has changed how people travel.
    c. people today can use technology to create art.
    d. art has changed technology.

2. How can technology change art?

    a. by changing how people talk about art
    b. by giving artists new ways to create art
    c. by designing computers that look like art
    d. by training artists to become computer experts

3. Name two ways technology is used in the arts today.

_____

_____

_____

Digital Photography

1. Another good name for "Digital Photography" might be _____

    a. "How to Take Digital Photographs."
    b. "Photography Becomes an Art Form."
    c. "Is Photography an Art Form?"
    d. "Famous Digital Photographs."

2. Why did people think photography was not art?

_____

_____

_____

3. How has photography changed over the years?

_____

_____

_____

Music and Computers

1. Why did some people think computers should not be used in music?

    a. They thought music on computers sounded bad.

    b. They thought music should be played on instruments.

    c. They thought music should only use real sounds.

    d. all of the above

2. What is a synthesizer?

_____

_____

_____

3. How can computers be used to compose music?

_____

_____

_____

Computer Art

1. "Computer Art" is MAINLY about _____

    a. how to put art on computers.

    b. how computers can design art.

    c. how artists use computers to create art.

    d. how many people buy and sell computer art.

2. In this reading, what does *technique* mean?

    a. creating digital paintings

    b. a way to use computers to paint

    c. using color in painting

    d. a way to do something

3. What is a stylus?

_____

_____

_____

technology	computer	photography	digital
musicians	synthesizer	technique	stylus

1. Choose the word from the word box above that best matches each definition. Write the word on the line below.

A. _____ people who make music

B. _____ a machine that can be used to store and use information

C. _____ a special kind of pen

D. _____ a way of doing things

E. _____ science that is used to make tools that people can use

F. _____ a way to create pictures

G. _____ relating to information that can be stored in a computer

H. _____ an electronic tool that can be used to make music and other sounds

2. Fill in the blanks in the sentences below. Choose the word from the word box that completes each sentence.

A. To create art on that computer, use the _____ to draw on that connected tablet.

B. Today, a _____ has replaced a pen and paper for many writers.

C. Some artists use a painting _____ that involves different sizes of brushes.

D. Both of those _____ play tubas.

E. The _____ camera stores pictures as computer files.

F. I can't tell if that music is a recording of live players or if it was done on a _____.

G. The car was a huge breakthrough in transportation _____.

H. Rena took up _____ so she would have a record of what her children looked like when they were young.

Art and Technology

1. Use the idea web to help you remember what you read. In each box, write the main idea of that reading.

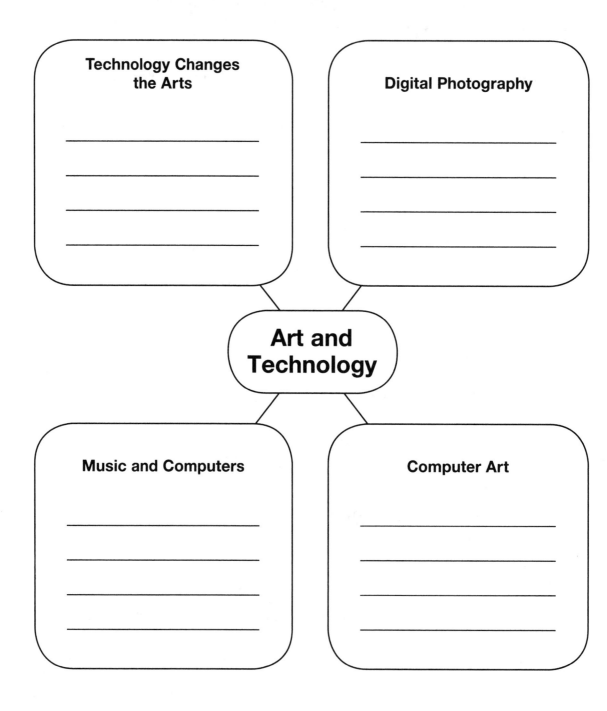

Technology Changes
the Arts

_____

_____

_____

_____

Digital Photography

_____

_____

_____

_____

**Art and
Technology**

Music and Computers

_____

_____

_____

_____

Computer Art

_____

_____

_____

_____

2. What did people first think about using technology in the arts?

_____

_____

_____

_____

3. How do artists use computers in music and painting today?

_____

_____

_____

_____

4. What are two ways the new technologies might change the art that artists make?

_____

_____

_____

_____

Fashion

New clothing designs come out each year.

Fast Facts

- About 62% of U.S. residents own more than ten T-shirts.

- A T-shirt was sold in the 1990s for $42,000 to raise money for charity.

- People in the United States spent more than $170 billion on clothing in 2004.

What Is Fashion?

Fashion is clothing that many people like to wear. The clothing that's fashionable changes, though. Every year,[20] designers sketch new clothing designs. Stores decide which designers' clothes people might like. Then, people go out and buy what has become the latest style.[45]

One example of how fashion catches on is the story of the T-shirt. It began its fashion as an undershirt for men in Europe.[69] United States soldiers saw the comfortable shirts during World War I. T-shirts caught on as men's underwear in the United States.[90]

By the 1950s, men were wearing T-shirts on the outside instead of as underwear. Movie stars started wearing them.[109] Today, many people wear T-shirts. Sometimes the shirts have words that tell about those wearing them. Many fans of sports[129] teams might wear shirts that tell which teams are those persons' favorites.[141]

KEY NOTES

What Is Fashion?
How did the T-shirt come into fashion?

_____

_____

Fashion

Traditional styles and designs influence fashion.

Fast Facts

- The first fashion magazine came out in 1586 in Germany.

- Some cloth in Africa is made from pounded bark.

- The word *kimono* first meant "clothing" in Japanese.

Where Fashion Comes From

Fashion designers get their ideas for new fashion from all over the world. In earlier centuries, for example, American[23] designers copied the latest fashions from Paris. Today, designers find ideas in other countries like Japan.[39]

One example of the worldwide trading of fashion ideas today is the influence of African style on designers from other[59] parts of the world. Designers from around the world use African cloth in their designs because they love its bold colors and[81] patterns. Some designers have copied traditional African draped clothing, including wrap skirts, and have designed jewelry that is influenced by African style.[103]

Another example of the trading of fashion ideas is the influence of the Japanese kimono in the work of designers from[124] Europe and the United States. Versions of the loose, flowing kimono can be seen in high-fashion clothing designed today.[144]

KEY NOTES

Where Fashion Comes From
Where does fashion come from?

_____

_____

Fashion

This fashion designer sketched her designs on a computer.

The Fashion Designer

The figure in the fashion world that people hear about is the designer. People with this career decide the shape and look of clothing most of us wear.[31]

First, a designer uses his or her imagination to come up with ideas for clothing designs. Ideas come from many places,[52] such as from the clothing of other countries and costumes in movies. Once the designer has an idea, he or she sketches the design for a piece of clothing.[81]

The next step is for the designer to turn that sketch into a pattern from which the clothing can be made. Then, people[104] whose career is sewing use the pattern to cut pieces of fabric and sew them into clothing. Finally, the clothing is ready to[127] go to stores, where buyers finally see the result of the designer's imagination.[140]

KEY NOTES

The Fashion Designer
What does a fashion designer do?

_____

_____

Fashion

The president of FUBU attends fashion shows.

Fast Facts

- About $450 million of FUBU clothing is sold each year.

- Today, FUBU designs and sells everything from bedding to shoes.

- FUBU's founders began their company with $5,000.

"For Us, By Us"

In 1992, several childhood friends from New York City decided to start a clothing company. They were *entrepreneurs*—[22] people who start a business. They wanted to design and sell clothing for people who wanted to look good in comfortable[43] clothing. Their clothing line was called "For Us, By Us"—FUBU. Today, FUBU helps set the style for hip-hop urban cool.[64]

The first products the company made were hats. Then, it added shirts. The entrepreneurs convinced hip-hop stars[81] to wear FUBU clothing. They felt that big companies did not respect the urban market. FUBU understood that many people[101] wanted to be part of that world, and the company's clothing soon became popular.[115]

At first, no big stores wanted FUBU's clothes, but they sold well in small stores. Today, FUBU clothing is available in stores big and small all over the world.[144]

KEY NOTES

For Us, By Us
Why did FUBU choose that name for the company?

_____

_____

Fashion

What Is Fashion?

1. One thing that is true of fashion is that _____

    a. it is designed for rich people.
    b. fashion always changes.
    c. T-shirts are not part of fashion.
    d. fashion designers do not like change.

2. The T-shirt was first _____

    a. only worn by women.
    b. worn as outerwear.
    c. worn as underwear.
    d. worn in the United States.

3. Tell how the T-shirt caught on as a fashion item.

_____

_____

_____

Where Fashion Comes From

1. The main idea of "Where Fashion Comes From" is _____

    a. fashion ideas come from around the world.
    b. ideas in fashion keep coming back.
    c. fashion once came from Europe.
    d. you can tell a person's country by his or her fashion.

2. How did African clothing influence global fashion design?

_____

_____

_____

3. How did Japan influence fashion designers?

_____

_____

_____

The Fashion Designer

1. "The Fashion Designer" is MAINLY about _____

    a. what fashion designers do.
    b. the many different stores that sell fashion.
    c. selling clothes for a living.
    d. how to get a job as a fashion designer.

2. What qualities does a good fashion designer need?

_____

_____

_____

3. What are three things a fashion designer does?

_____

_____

_____

"For Us, By Us"

1. Another good name for "For Us, By Us" is _____

  a. "Urban Fashion Entrepreneurs."
  b. "Selling Clothes in Cities."
  c. "New York City Clothes."
  d. "Urban Music and Fashion."

2. How did FUBU first get people interested in its clothes?

_____

_____

_____

3. FUBU sets the style for _____

  a. people who like music.
  b. people who live near cities.
  c. people who like urban cool.
  d. people who make music.

172

fashion	designer	influence	kimono
career	imagination	urban	entrepreneur

1. Choose the word from the word box above that best matches each definition. Write the word on the line below.

A. _____ a person who starts a business

B. _____ the act of creating new images or ideas

C. _____ what a person does to earn a living

D. _____ one who thinks up and draws plans

E. _____ a Japanese robe

F. _____ the style of dressing

G. _____ the power to act on or affect persons or things

H. _____ having to do with cities

2. Fill in the blanks in the sentences below. Choose the word from the word box that completes each sentence.

A. She wore her _____ from Japan as a jacket.

B. I always buy the latest _____ because I like to dress well.

C. An _____ area always has more buildings than do places in the country.

D. That _____ likes to make clothing that is simple.

E. I can see the _____ of Asian design in the shape of that ring.

F. A good clothing designer needs _____ to make up new designs.

G. That _____ started a company that sells a new kind of cloth.

H. I am looking to train for a _____ in clothing design.

173

Fashion

1. Use the idea web to help you remember what you read. In each box, write the main idea of that reading.

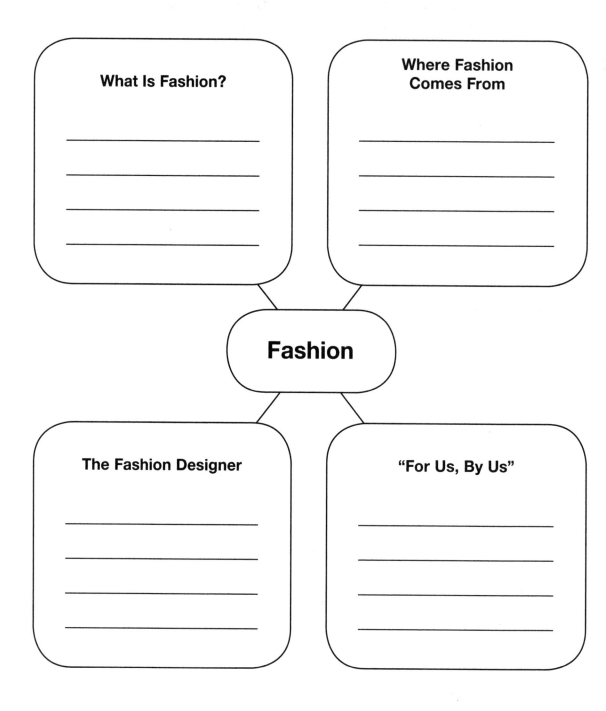

What Is Fashion?

_____

_____

_____

_____

Where Fashion Comes From

_____

_____

_____

_____

Fashion

The Fashion Designer

_____

_____

_____

"For Us, By Us"

_____

_____

_____

2. Tell two facts you learned about fashion in these readings.

_____

_____

_____

_____

3. Why do you think fashion designers use elements from around the world?

_____

_____

_____

_____

4. If you were a fashion designer, what influences would you use to design your clothing?

_____

_____

_____

_____

Acknowledgments

Photo Credits

Cover photos: (top) BananaStock/Punchstock; (bottom, L-R) Stockbyte Silver/Getty Images; Comstock Images/Punchstock; Digital Vision/Punchstock; Dave Bartruff/Digital Vision/Getty Images; **Page:** 8 Elizabeth Holms/Omni-Photo Communications, Inc.; 10 Courtesy of the Library of Congress; 12 Edwin Levick/Hulton Archive/Getty Images; 14 © Spencer Grant/Photo Edit, Inc.; 22 © Dennis MacDonald/PhotoEdit; 24 Mark Downey/Photodisc Green/Getty Images; 26 © David R. Frazier/Photolibrary, Inc.; 28 Bruna Stude/Omni-Photo Communications, Inc.; 36 Gavin Hellier/Robert Harding; 38 The Roman army crossing the Danube, detail from Trajan's Column, 113 AD (limestone), Roman (2nd cent. AD)/Giraudon, The Forum, Rome, Italy/The Bridgeman Art Library; 40 © David Buffington/age footstock; 42 The Art Archive/Museo della Civiltà Romana, Rome/Dagli Orti; 50 © Bettmann/Corbis; 52 © Bettmann/Corbis; 54 © Aaron Horowitz/Corbis; 56 © Bettmann/Corbis; 64 © Mark Richards/PhotoEdit; 66 Ron Chapple/Taxi/Getty Images; 68 © Bob Daemmrich/Stock Boston; 70 Victor Habbick Visions/Photo Researchers, Inc.; 78 © Robert Brenner/PhotoEdit; 80 © PhotoAlto/SuperStock; 82 Goodby, Silverstein & Partners; 84 Photodisc/Punchstock; 92 © Jose Carillo/PhotoEdit; 94 © John W. Karapelou, CMI/Phototake. All rights reserved.; 96 Andy Crawford © Dorling Kindersley; 98 © Michael Newman/PhotoEdit; 106 Michael P. Doukas/U.S. Geological Survey, David A. Johnston, Cascades Volcano Observatory; 108 National Geophysical Data Center; 110 PhotoDisc/Getty Images; 112 Peter French/PacificStock.com; 120 John Serafin; 122 PhotoDisc/Getty Images; 124 Carl Shaneff/PacificStock.com; 126 Argus/Peter Arnold, Inc.; 134 Jonathan Elderfield/Getty Images; 136 Nick Kleinberg/Corbis; 138 AP Images; 140 Wesley Hitt/Mira.com; 148 Maximilian Stock Ltd./Photo Researchers, Inc.; 150 © Randy Faris/Corbis; 152 © Jack Hollingsworth/Corbis; 154 © TWPhoto/Corbis. All Rights Reserved.; 162 © Michael Newman/PhotoEdit; 164 © Rob Howard/Corbis. All Rights Reserved.; 166 Digital Vision/Getty Images; 168 Getty Images

Text Credits

• "The Raven" by Edgar Allan Poe. 1845. *Selected Poetry and Prose of Poe.* Ed. T.O. Mabbott. Copyright © 1951 by Random House, Inc. New York: Random House/The Modern Library. Dist. by McGraw-Hill, Inc.
• "The Tell-Tale Heart" by Edgar Allan Poe. 1843. *The Complete Tales and Poems of Edgar Allen Poe.* Barnes & Noble, Inc., by arrangement with Alfred A. Knopf, Inc. © 1992. All rights reserved.

Staff Credits

Members of the AMP™ QReads™ team: Melania Benzinger, Karen Blonigen, Carol Bowling, Michelle Carlson, Kazuko Collins, Nancy Condon, Barbara Drewlo, Sue Gulsvig, Daren Hastings, Laura Henrichsen, Ruby Hogen-Chin, Julie Johnston, Mary Kaye Kuzma, Julie Maas, Daniel Milowski, Carrie O'Connor, Julie Theisen, Mary Verrill, Mike Vineski, Charmaine Whitman